MUM'S SNEAKY RECIPES

200 creative ways to smuggle fruit and vegetables into delicious meals for children

Samantha Quinn

ROBINSON

ROBINSON

First published in Great Britain in 2017 by Robinson

A CIP catalogue record for this book is available from the British Library.

ISBN: 978-1-47213-909-2

Typeset by Basement Press, Glaisdale
Printed and bound in Great Britain by Clays Ltd, St Ives plc

Papers used by Robinson are from well-managed forests and other responsible sources.

MIX
Paper from
responsible sources
FSC® C104740

Robinson
An imprint of
Little, Brown Book Group
Carmelite House
50 Victoria Embankment
London EC4Y 0DZ

An Hachette UK Company
www.hachette.co.uk

www.littlebrown.co.uk

How To Books are published by Robinson, an imprint of Little, Brown Book Group. We welcome proposals from authors who have first-hand experience of their subjects. Please set out the aims of your book, its target market and its suggested contents in an email to
Nikki.Read@howtobooks.co.uk

The recommendations given in this book are solely intended as education and should not be taken as medical advice.

CONTENTS

PREFACE

One of the concepts behind this book came as a result of my toddler refusing to eat anything apart from a dull array of beige-coloured foods. Over time I became concerned about my son's nutrient intake and soon realised I needed to invent a fun, new, exciting way to entice him to eat his greens. I soon discovered endless ways of sneaking fruit and veg into delicious meals for my children. It not only worked for my toddler, it worked wonders for my older children too! I created imaginative recipes that I could present alongside stories and games to help encourage them to eat more nutritious meals. I truly believe that encouraging children to eat a nutritious, healthy, well-balanced diet from an early age is important for a number of reasons. It keeps them more energised, supports their ability to learn and educates them on making healthier food choices in later life.

The recipes and ideas in this book will help you introduce healthier eating habits so that your family eat nutritious foods at any time of the day or year. Recipe ideas range from brilliant breakfasts to perfect party food. There is also a chapter dedicated to superfoods to boost children's intake of essential nutrients for energy and growth. This book will help families bond during mealtimes and encourage healthy-eating habits that can be passed on to the next generation. I love the fact that it was my children who inspired me to create these recipes. My need to do right by my children introduced me to a rich world of fascinating ideas that I couldn't be without today.

CONVERSION CHARTS

Weight

Metric	Imperial
25g	1oz
50g	2oz
75g	3oz
100g	4oz
150g	5oz
175g	6oz
200g	7oz
225g	8oz
250g	9oz
300g	10oz
350g	12oz
400g	14oz
450g	1lb

Oven temperatures

Celsius	Fahrenheit
110°C	225°F
120°C	250°F
140°C	275°F
150°C	300°F
160°C	325°F
180°C	350°F
190°C	375°F
200°C	400°F
220°C	425°F
230°C	450°F
240°C	475°F

Liquids

Metric	Imperial	US cup
5ml	1 tsp	1 tsp
15ml	1 tbsp	1 tbsp
50ml	2fl oz	3 tbsp
60ml	2½fl oz	¼ cup
75ml	3fl oz	⅓ cup
100ml	4fl oz	scant ½ cup
125ml	4½fl oz	½ cup
150ml	5fl oz	⅔ cup
200ml	7fl oz	scant 1 cup
250ml	9fl oz	1 cup
300ml	½pt	1¼ cup
350ml	12fl oz	1⅓ cup
400ml	¾pt	1¾ cup
500ml	17fl oz	2 cups
600ml	1pt	2½ cup

Measurements

Metric	Imperial
5cm	2in
10cm	4in
13cm	5in
15cm	6in
18cm	7in
20cm	8in
25cm	10in
30cm	12in

1
INTRODUCTION: GETTING READY TO BE A SNEAKY MUM

I REMEMBER IT WELL . . .

. . . popping my little boy into his high chair to offer him his first taste of solid food . . . Beaming with joy as I watched him sink his little gums into my premium selection of puréed wonder-foods, including fresh fruits, vegetables and pulses . . . Oh, the exhilaration of every successful mealtime! I felt proud (and lucky!) that my little one's diverse palate allowed him to enjoy nutrient-rich foods that would help him grow and thrive . . .

I also felt bemused by other mums who constantly bemoaned their beloved 'picky eaters'! What had caused their otherwise delightful offspring to adopt strange, restrictive diets? Why did they flatly refuse to try any new foods? What on earth were these mums talking about? My son relished all his meals!

A BUMPY LANDING

My smugness was indeed short-lived. In fact, I returned from Cloud Nine back to Planet Earth around the time of my son's second birthday. I have no idea what was in his birthday cake that day, but he joined the above-mentioned 'Picky Eaters Club' almost overnight! My eager little boy would henceforth eat only dippy eggs and a dull array of beige-coloured foods such as chips and toasted soldiers.

GAME ON

Like any mum who encounters her child's sudden, self-imposed food denial, I responded with growing anxiety and concern. I became anxious about my son's nutrient intake and concerned for his wellbeing. However, like all mums, child-rearing has also prepped me to develop quick-thinking skills and rapid-response techniques. I decided to avoid all confrontation over my son's restrictive food choices. I remained, however, determined that he would continue to eat a well-balanced diet that included his 'Five-a-Day' portions of fruits and vegetables.

How did I achieve this? Well, they say that necessity is the mother of invention and I certainly became the mother who needed to invent! My head began to whirl with ideas for healthy recipes that would please my pernickety toddler. I discovered endless ways of sneaking fruit or veggie portions into his meals and snacks. I began to create a collection of sneaky recipes from yummy smoothies to tasty soups – and my son devoured them because there wasn't a fruit or vegetable in sight. (They were all blended to invisible perfection for my little prince to enjoy.) I WAS WINNING!

THE GAME CHANGER

Despite my apparent 'success', something didn't feel quite right. My sneaky recipes enabled me to create wholesome meals that my son devoured. However, if I continued to hide and disguise the fruits and vegetables that my son clearly enjoyed eating, how would he know that he actually enjoyed eating them? And I wanted to avoid a silent agreement with my son's view that fruit and veg were somehow 'yukky' and should be avoided at all costs. I found a very simple solution. I simply placed fruits and vegetables onto his plate alongside his prepared 'sneaky' meal so that he could see them, touch them and taste them if he wanted to. If he didn't – no worries! I'd already sneaked some into his meal anyway!

Strangely enough, once I relaxed, my son did too. Once he felt that he had full control over his own food choices, he became more adventurous and less fussy with every passing week. My relaxed attitude to my son's eating has certainly paid dividends in that he has transformed from a fussy little toddler into a smart little boy who enjoys eating healthy foods. He loves to potter about with me in the kitchen and he has even helped me create some of the recipes in this book.

HOME COOKING

The maxim 'We are what we eat' rings loud and true when applied to our children. Well-nourished children have boundless energy (without being hyperactive). They are mentally alert and they sleep soundly. In addition, a well-balanced diet promotes healthy growth and development and a strong immune system that can fight colds and flu.

Cooking at home with your kids is a fun way for them to learn about food groups and feel encouraged to try new foods. Cooking meals from scratch also gives you more control over additives, sugar and salt.

Home cooking enables you to create meals that are cheaper, tastier and more nutritious than ready-prepared or takeaway options. What's not to love?

FEEDING YOUR CHILDREN A BALANCED DIET

A balanced diet that contains essential nutrients for growth and development helps keep kids happy and healthy. But what comprises a well-balanced daily diet for children?

- One portion of a carbohydrate food, such as bread, rice or pasta, at every mealtime.
- Two to three portions of protein foods, such as eggs, beans and fish every day.
- Two to three portions of dairy foods, such as milk, cheese and yoghurt, daily.
- At least five portions of fruits and vegetables – yep, that's a rainbow five-a-day!

Children should eat three meals a day. Breakfast is an especially important meal for kids of all ages and shouldn't be skipped. A wholesome breakfast is even more essential for kids who attend nursery or school because it will help maintain their levels of energy and concentration until lunchtime. Being away from home gives your child restricted mealtimes; this makes breakfast a top priority and will keep hunger locked up until lunch.

MENU MUST-HAVES

Carbohydrates

Children are inquisitive, bouncy little souls who need small, regular portions of carbohydrate foods for sustained energy throughout the day. There are two types of carbohydrates: simple and complex. Simple carbohydrates are present in processed, starchy and sugary products such as white bread, biscuits and cakes. Complex carbohydrates are found in foods that contain wholegrains, such as wholemeal bread and oaty breakfast cereals. While simple carbs can provide a quick energy boost, complex carbohydrates provide a slower and more sustained boost as they take a little longer to digest. Wholegrain carbs often contain a greater variety of vitamins and minerals, along with fibre, to help maintain a healthy digestive system.

Proteins

Protein foods provide the building blocks for your child's healthy growth and development. Protein comprises long chains of substances called amino acids, of which around twenty have so far been identified and named, including *arginine, lysine* and *tryptophan (tryptophan can also improve your child's sleep; a bonus in itself)*. Of these twenty amino acids, ten are considered *essential* components of a healthy diet because they are not produced by the body and must therefore be obtained from food. Foods such as meat, eggs and fish are sources of *complete protein*, which means they provide the full range of essential amino acids. Plant foods such as nuts, seeds, grains and beans are considered sources of *incomplete protein* because they lack one or more of the essential amino acids needed by the body. (However, soya products such as soya milk may contain the full range of essential amino acids because the humble soya bean is actually a *complete protein.*)

Vegetarians and vegans can obtain *complementary complete protein* from their diets by combining two or more sources of incomplete protein. For example, a nutritious vegetarian daily menu might comprise of a bowl of cereal such as muesli with milk for breakfast; baked beans on wholemeal toast topped with a sprinkling of grated cheese for lunch, and wholemeal pasta with a lentil and vegetable sauce for supper.

The recipes in this book will show you ways to combine foods to ensure that your child is offered delicious meals that provide complete protein.

Fats

Fats are important to a healthy diet as they perform essential functions within the body such as protecting organs, building tissues and carrying fat-soluble vitamins such as vitamins A and D. Children are rapidly growing and developing; they have high energy needs and yet they can only take in and digest a small volume of food at each mealtime or snack time. Therefore, fats provide an important source of concentrated energy for young children and, for this reason, children should be offered full-fat products such as whole milk unless otherwise directed by a doctor or health-care provider.

There are different types of fat, which are classified as either saturated or unsaturated. Foods high in saturated fat include butter, cream, cheese and processed meats such as sausages. Unsaturated fats are further classified into monounsaturated or polyunsaturated fats and these can be obtained from foods such as plant-based oils, avocados, nuts, seeds and fish. Omega-3 is a type of polyunsaturated fatty acid that is found abundantly in foods such as oily fish (for example, salmon and sardines) and in smaller quantities in foods such as egg yolk, flaxseed and linseed. Sufficient intake of omega-3 seems to be particularly important for infants and toddlers to enable visual acuity and healthy development of organs such as the brain.

Diets high in saturated fats are linked with the development of health problems such as high cholesterol, whereas both types of unsaturated fats can help lower blood cholesterol levels when used instead of saturated fat and as part of a well-balanced eating plan. Therefore, although young children should eat full-fat rather than low-fat varieties of foods such as yoghurts, it's important for the sake of their future health to avoid giving them a constant supply of 'junk' foods that are high in saturated fat. Junk foods such as crisps, cakes, biscuits, pastries, chocolate, sausages, beefburgers and pizza are usually high in additives such as salt and sugar and often provide limited nutritional value. Now, the idea of a 'junk food addiction' might seem far-fetched when applied to a toddler, but junk foods are habit-forming. Children can get used to the overwhelming fatty texture and sugary or salty flavours of processed foods to the point where they refuse to eat anything that tastes fresh and natural. A good example of this would be if a child cannot eat a scrumptious, freshly picked, tangy strawberry without dipping it in sugar first!

SING A RAINBOW – EAT A RAINBOW!

This book contains lists of vitamins and minerals that are essential for your child's healthy growth and development. Many of these nutrients can easily be obtained by simply eating at least five portions of different-coloured fruits and vegetables each day. Here's an example of a simple one-day 'rainbow' meal-planner for your child:

Breakfast
Bowl of porridge made with milk and with a handful of blueberries stirred in (one portion)
Glass of orange juice (one portion)

Snack
An apple and a piece of cheese (one portion)

Lunch
Bowl of lentil and red pepper soup (one portion)
Wholemeal bread roll
Banana (one portion)

Snack
Fruit smoothie made with milk, yoghurt and a handful of frozen berries (one portion)
Oatcake spread with smooth nut butter

Dinner
Fish pie with broccoli, carrots and frozen peas (three portions)
Fresh peach slices with ice cream (one portion)

As you can see from this meal-planner, a 'rainbow five-a-day' can easily be achieved through a colourful combination of fruits and vegetables that are dried, canned, frozen and fresh. Fruit juice counts as one portion, but can only count as a portion once a day. (For example, having five glasses of orange juice in one day would not meet the five-a-day recommendations!)

A NOTE ABOUT FIBRE

Fibre is found in fruits, vegetables and wholegrains. A healthy diet that includes adequate amounts of fibre enables the smooth transit of food through the digestive system. Lack of fibre and an insufficient fluid intake are the two main causes of constipation. A sluggish digestive system, coupled with bouts of painful constipation, is enough to make any one of us feel exhausted and irritable – and your child is no exception!

However, a healthy lifestyle is often achieved through an approach that is a moderate rather than extreme. Along with discomfort caused by a lack of fibre, too much fibre in your child's diet could also cause problems. The UK Foods Standards Agency recommends a slow and gradual introduction of high-fibre starchy foods such as wholemeal bread and brown rice so that your toddler/child doesn't become full too soon and before he or she has eaten enough calories.

'A high-fibre diet is more bulky, which means it could fill up your child too quickly so they don't get all the energy they need. And too much fibre can sometimes reduce the amount of minerals a child can absorb, such as calcium and iron.' (The UK Food Standards Agency) (from 'Feeding Your Toddler', found under the 'Nutrition Publications' section on the Food Standards Agency website)

FOOD, GLORIOUS FOOD!

The recipes in this book focus upon simple ways to sneak lots of lovely colourful fruits and veggies into your child's meals and snacks. However, it's also important to remain aware of the bigger picture, which involves empowering your child to make his or her own independent, healthy food choices.

The next section describes simple ways to help you steer your child towards a well-balanced diet without any need for coaxing, nagging or sneaking. One day you will look at your child in amazement as you suddenly realise that a plateful of broccoli has been devoured for the second time in a week!

Until then, please use these recipes as a way of ensuring that your child gets the nourishment he or she needs and deserves, resulting in improved moods and optimum physical and cognitive development.

MUM'S TIPS FOR HAPPY, HEALTHY MEALTIMES!

Set an example

You can often predict children's future eating behaviours simply by observing the eating patterns of their parents. If healthy foods such as fruits and vegetables are no more than an afterthought in your household, it's unlikely that your kids will enjoy them and make them a priority. On the other hand, if your kids see you quite naturally picking up an apple instead of a biscuit or nibbling on a handful of dried raisins instead of crisps, then the chances are they will follow suit without even thinking about it.

It's also a good idea to eat together as a family whenever possible. Relaxed family mealtimes give you a chance to bond with your kids and chat about the day's events and other topics. This can help take the pressure off your child and what he or she is eating, enabling everyone to enjoy food at their own pace and of their own accord.

Foodie adventures

Kids love to play make-believe games. Why not add a little gentle fun to your mealtimes? This doesn't mean letting your kids 'play with their food' or forget basic table manners. Instead, a little humour and imaginative play can transform a potentially tense and tricky situation into a more agreeable atmosphere. For example, if your child finds broccoli florets too intimidating, you might describe them as little tree snacks for hungry dinosaurs. (You could also sneak some broccoli into your kid's beloved pasta dish using our 'colourful pasta' recipe!) You can make 'smiley face' pancakes, use cookie cutters to turn toast into stars, hearts and teddies, while raisins and celery can become 'ants on a log'. You're usually onto a winner with anything 'mini'! (Petit Pois that want to go to a party in your belly? Bring it on!) Playing little make-believe games that form a link between healthy foods and things that your child already loves are a simple way to get a few bites of greens 'down the hatch'.

Kids in the kitchen

Children love to help out with culinary tasks such as grating a carrot, slicing a banana, mixing a dressing or pressing the button on a blender. Cooking is a great way to bond with your kids and they enjoy tasting the results of their efforts, so it's a win-win situation! Letting kids help out with tasks such as setting the table gives them a sense of pride and encourages greater enthusiasm and cooperation at mealtimes. You could also take your children along to farmers' markets or grocery stores where they can choose a couple of things to cook for dinner. Maybe pick a curious-looking vegetable that can be chopped up into a veggie casserole or an exotic fruit that you can try out in a juicy fruit salad? Better still, create a little 'grow your own' garden area where kids can plant and harvest their own supplies. If you have little space, why not let your kids plant herbs in pots that you can place on a sun-drenched windowsill? Many types of veg such as spinach and carrots can also be grown in containers. The possibilities are endless!

Get dipping

When you are trying to encourage children to taste different kinds of vegetables, it's a great idea to place dips alongside your veggie selection. Children feel in control and become more willing to try new textures and flavours when they can pick and dip independently. Why not let your child help you prepare some dips? You could also focus upon colours by serving up a rainbow of vegetables on the plate. For example, create an arc shape of red peppers, orange carrots, yellow peppers, green celery and purple asparagus. You can make dips in lots of different colours, too, for your child to explore and enjoy.

Add to the fun by playing the 'Dipping Guessing Game'. This game is ideal if your child is an extremely fussy eater and it's the way I got my little boy to take his first taste of vegetables. To begin with, place a blindfold over your eyes. Let your child select a veg stick, dunk it into a chosen dip and then pop it into your mouth. You can make this really fun by expressing your pleasure as you try to guess which vegetable has been chosen and which dip has been used. 'Wow – this tastes amazing! Is it Mummy's yummy hummus and Rabby rabbit's favourite carrot?' Once your child sees how much fun you're having, he or she may feel prompted to have a go.

Don't force them to finish . . .

Using ultimatums or threats to get children to eat the food in front of them is usually a big mistake. By all means turn off the TV and put the iPad away to get rid of unnecessary distractions while you are eating. However, punishments such as disallowing a favourite TV programme because your child's plate wasn't cleared creates unnecessary negative associations with food. If your child is a picky eater, negative food experiences are likely to heighten anxiety and cause further food rejection. Healthy eating begins with a healthy attitude: stay relaxed, feel positive and have fun.

. . . But praise them when they try!

The 'other side of the coin' is, of course, that relaxed and positive experiences around food can help *reduce* picky-eating tendencies.

Rewarding a child with a smile, a hug, positive comments and perhaps a little sticker now and again for trying just one bite of a rejected food is likely to encourage a curious attitude towards new foods and the development of a healthy appetite.

A child's world

Children function using a different set of values to those that adults often hold dear. Young children are usually unconcerned by thoughts about their own state of health – indeed many toddlers actually believe they are invincible! So telling children that a particular food is 'healthy' might not persuade them that it's worth tasting. On the other hand, many children can feel limited by their size and wish to become bigger and stronger. Therefore, simply stating that 'broccoli helps you grow big and strong' is usually more effective than 'it's healthy' or 'eat it because I said so'.

De-junk your larder – and your mind

Simply stated, it's you and not your child who holds the purse strings and you have responsibility for which foods fill up your kitchen cupboards, fridge and freezer. Provide fewer junk food snacks for your children to graze on and you'll find them seeking out healthier alternatives such as fruits, vegetables, yoghurts and wholegrains.

At the same time, it's important to keep a sense of perspective and to occasionally let your children indulge in a few sweet treats, salty snacks or creamy desserts. Having popcorn at the movies, some candyfloss at the seaside, a carton of chips while out shopping or a chocolate lolly from an ice cream van form part of life's 'foody' pleasures. As long as you tip the balance mostly in favour of smart food choices and regular physical activity, your kids will be fine.

Breakfast like a (little) king, queen or princess!

You've heard it *so* many times before, but it's always worth stating again because it is *so* important. A nutritious breakfast gives your child the best possible start to the day. A healthy, well-balanced breakfast improves children's mental performance and concentration and provides energy for the morning's activities. Children who skip breakfast are more sluggish and less attentive, which is not good news for their overall growth, learning and development. Indeed, teachers have observed that children who come to school hungry experience more learning difficulties than well-nourished children.

Studies show that children who eat breakfast perform much better in their school work than their non-breakfast-eating peers and they also have enough energy left over to get involved in extra-curricular sports activities such as football and gymnastics.

2
BEAMING BREAKFASTS

Your child is likely to have a good appetite in the morning having spent many hours sleeping and without any food intake. It's therefore a good idea to make the most of breakfast time and use it as a chance to include extra fruits or health foods for optimum nutrition. This chapter includes a selection of tasty recipes that will appeal to your toddler's sense of fun and deliver powerful nutrients and fuel for the best part of the day.

APPLE DELIGHT BITES

It's worth remembering that old adage 'An apple a day keeps the doctor away'. Apples are loaded with nutrients such as vitamin C and they also contain an antioxidant called quercetin, which might help boost the immune system and keep your little one feeling bright and bouncy. Apples contain useful amounts of fibre too. Kids seem to like the sweet-tart taste of apples, so 'appley' recipes such as this one are usually very well received!

To create these fun fruit sandwiches, simply slice some apples horizontally and remove their cores. Then spread with some lovely Homemade Peanut Butter (instructions given below) and sprinkle with cinnamon.

HOMEMADE PEANUT BUTTER

Prep time: 5 minutes
Cooking time: 15 minutes

250g raw peanuts
3 tbsp coconut oil
2 tsp honey
1 banana, chopped

- Preheat the oven to 180°C/Gas Mark 4.
- Place the peanuts onto a baking tray in a single layer and add the coconut oil. Roast the peanuts in the oven for 15 minutes, turning every 5 minutes to make sure they are evenly coated and do not burn.
- Remove the peanuts from the oven and put them to one side to cool. Once cooled, place the peanuts into a food processor then add the honey. Blend the ingredients until smooth, then add the chopped banana and blend for about a minute. Spread desired amount onto the apple. Place leftover spread in a container and pop in the fridge for future use.

Mum's Tip: Don't forget to sprinkle on a little cinnamon! Cinnamon contains health-boosting antioxidant flavonoids which have antibacterial and anti-inflammatory properties.

APRICOT AND CRANBERRY CEREAL BARS

Homemade cereal bars make healthy, energy-boosting snacks for breakfast and beyond and kids seem to love their crunchy texture and biscuity taste. Try making these bars on a Sunday and you'll have a stock of healthy breakfasts and snack options ready for your family's hectic week ahead.

Makes 12 bars
Prep time: 10 minutes
Cooking time: 20 minutes

200g porridge oats
100g sunflower seeds
50g pine nuts
50g chopped walnuts
50g dried cranberries
50g chopped apricots
125g butter
4 tbsp honey
1 tsp cinnamon
75g light brown sugar

- Preheat the oven to 180°C/Gas Mark 4.
- Mix together the oats, seeds, fruit and nuts in a bowl and set aside.
- Place the butter, honey, cinnamon and sugar into a pan and heat gently, stirring all the time until melted.
- Remove the pan from the heat and stir in the oats, seeds, nuts and fruit. Mix well.
- Grease and line the base of a baking tray.
- Transfer the mixture to the lined baking tray. Spread evenly and press down firmly with the back of a spoon. Bake in the oven for 20 minutes or until golden-brown.
- Once baked, allow to cool before cutting and lifting the bars out of the tray.

Mum's Tip: I usually lay a piece of baking paper over the top of the mixture. Then I get another pan and press down hard – it helps seal the ingredients together.

BERRY EXPLOSION MILKSHAKE

Delicious, deep-coloured berries have a high antioxidant count to boost healthy development and a strong immune system. Berries taste succulent and sweet and their vibrant colours add to the fun of blending them into milkshakes and smoothies.

Serves 2
Prep time: 5–10 minutes

750ml milk
2 bananas, chopped
50g blueberries
50g strawberries
1 tsp honey

- Pour the milk into a blender. Add the bananas and process until liquidised. Add the blueberries, strawberries and honey and blend again until combined.

Mum's Tip: Honey is not only delicious, it also contains natural anti-viral and antibacterial agents for health and healing. So add a spoonful to reap the benefits.

BLUEBERRY BREAKFAST MUFFINS

These sweet muffins are filled with blueberry goodness and are perfect if you need a breakfast that you can grab and go!

Makes 12 muffins
Prep time: 10 minutes
Cooking time: 25 minutes

cooking oil spray
115g butter
110g brown sugar
1 banana, mashed
110ml milk
1 tsp vanilla extract
2 eggs
150g wholemeal flour
80g wheat bran
1 tsp baking powder
1-3 tbsp chopped walnuts
100g blueberries

- Preheat oven to 190°C/Gas Mark 5.
- Coat a 12-cup muffin tray with cooking oil spray.
- Place the butter and sugar into a large bowl and whisk until the texture is fluffy and creamy. Add the banana, milk, vanilla extract and eggs and mix well.
- Combine the flour, wheat bran and baking powder and blend into the banana mixture. Stir in the amount of walnuts you require and then pour the mixture into the muffin tray.
- Bake for 20-25 minutes or until a toothpick inserted into the centre of the muffin comes out clean.
- Leave to cool in the tray for 5 minutes and then place on a wire rack to cool completely.

PRETTY PINK PRINCESS PORRIDGE/
INCREDIBLE HULK PORRIDGE ....

Breakfasts that contain oats are ideal for children. Oats contain soluble fibre and protein to help keep little tummies full on long school mornings. Adding some nutrient-dense strawberries to the mix transforms a creamy-beige breakfast into pretty pink porridge – perfect for your little princess!

Serves 1–2
Prep time: 5 minutes
Cooking time: 10 minutes

40g porridge oats
280ml milk
40g strawberries

- Follow the manufacturer's instructions for cooking the porridge with the milk.
- Chop the strawberries and blend with a tablespoon of milk, then swirl the fruity liquid into the porridge mixture. Or pop in a handful of spinach (with a little honey) for Hulk power!

Mum's Tip: My girls used to love this story about a princess and her magical porridge!

'Yasmin was an ordinary princess who lived in an ordinary palace. She always ate plain, ordinary porridge for her breakfast. Then, one morning, a fairy godmother flew in through the palace window and swirled some pink, juicy crushed strawberries into Yasmin's porridge ... When Yasmin saw the porridge she ate it at once. It tasted delicious and it gave her magical powers! Yasmin kept her magical powers a secret so that no one knew what would happen every time she ate pink fruity porridge for her breakfast. Can you guess what powers she had?'

Then spend a little while discussing the magic powers breakfast may give you.

SPECIAL BAKED BEANS ON TOAST ....

Beans give a power-packed punch to the start of the day. A nutrient-packed superfood your little ones will love.

Serves 4
Prep time: 10 minutes
Cooking time: 10 minutes

1 red onion, diced
½ tsp extra-virgin olive oil
1 carrot, grated
1 red pepper, diced
1 garlic clove, sliced
1 can chopped tomatoes
(400g)
1 can cannellini beans
(380g)
1 can kidney beans (380g)
salt and pepper to taste
pinch of parsley
handful of grated Cheddar
cheese, optional

- Place the red onion into a medium-sized pan and gently fry in a little oil.
- Add the carrot and red pepper to the pan and fry for 5 minutes, stirring continuously. Add the garlic and cook for a further minute.
- Then add the tomatoes and beans, season and cook for 5 minutes.
- Serve on wholemeal toast with a sprinkle of parsley and grated cheese, if required.

Mum's Tip: I love adding a little sprinkle of grated cheese to this dish.

STRAWBERRY SURPRISE PANCAKES ....

These pancakes are sweet tasting but oh-so-healthy.

Makes 4 pancakes
Prep time: 5 minutes
Cooking time: 10 minutes

100g plain flour
2 eggs
250ml milk
6 strawberries
1 banana, chopped
butter
brown sugar, to serve

- Place the flour, eggs and milk into a blender, pulse for a few moments. Then blend in the strawberries and banana.
- Set a medium-sized frying pan over a medium heat setting. When the pan is hot, add a little butter, pour the pancake mixture into the centre of the pan to form a circular blob of mixture.
- Cook for 2–3 minutes on each side.
- Sprinkle with brown sugar to serve.
- Repeat the method until you have made 4 pancakes.

TEDDY'S BLUEBERRY TOAST

Blueberries come top of many lists of so-called 'superfoods' and this is because they are rich in vitamins, phytochemicals and soluble fibre. Ideal superfood for your mini superhero!

Prep time: 10 minutes
Chilling time: 30 minutes

60ml coconut milk
85g chopped apricots
2 tsp chia seeds
320g fresh blueberries
50g strawberries
1 tsp honey
1tsp coconut sugar (or
  granulated sugar)
1 slice wholemeal toast,
  shaped using a teddy-
  shaped cutter

- Pour the coconut milk into the blender and add the apricots.
- Blend on a high speed, until the apricots have broken up.
- Add the chia seeds, coconut sugar and half of the blueberries. Pulse the mixture on a low setting a few times to break up the berries.
- Add the strawberries and remaining blueberries and pulse a few times on low to create a thick, chunky consistency.
- Stir in a little honey, but avoid adding too much as it will make the jam too runny.
- Chill in the fridge for 30 minutes. The chia seeds will thicken the jam and the flavours will develop.
- This jam will keep in the fridge for up to 4 days.
- Make toast and spread when desired.

Mum's Tip: Chia seeds are rich in omega-3 fatty acids and they also contain protein, fibre, antioxidants and other essential nutrients such as calcium – ideal for growing little bodies.

TROPICAL FRUIT SALAD

Creating art using pieces of food is a fun way to help entice your kids to eat their five-a-day.

Prep time: 10 minutes

1 tangerine
1 banana
1 kiwi fruit
¼ pineapple
3 red grapes, deseeded and halved

- This tropical island food art has tangerine segments at the base of the tree, banana slices as tree trunks, kiwi half-slices as tropical leaves and pineapple cut into the shape of a sun. Some red grapes hanging from the trees complete the picture!

Mum's Tip: It's a great idea to get kids to help prepare food art. It's a great creative exercise which kids love!

VEGGIE BREAKFAST MUFFINS

Eggs provide ideal food for growing kids as they are full of protein, essential fats and nutrients such as vitamin B12. Mushrooms are also very nutritious, providing B vitamins, along with minerals such as copper and potassium.

Makes 12 muffins
Prep time: 10 minutes
Cooking time: 20 minutes

half a small red onion, finely diced
half a red pepper, diced
50g baby mushrooms, diced
1 tbsp rapeseed oil
4 large eggs
1 tbsp milk
50g Cheddar cheese, grated
salt and pepper

- Preheat the oven at 200°C/Gas Mark 6.
- Fry the onion, pepper and mushrooms in the oil for 3–5 minutes.
- Meanwhile, whisk together the eggs, milk and cheese in a large bowl.
- Once the vegetables are softened, add the egg mixture to the pan, add salt and pepper and mix well.
- Grease pan and divide the mixture into the sections of a 12-cup non-stick muffin pan and bake for 15 minutes.

VEGGIE EGG BREAKFAST WRAP

Red peppers are the worthy sidekicks of the green leafy family. They are abundant in the B-complex family group of vitamins such as niacin, pyridoxine (vitamin B6), riboflavin, and thiamin (vitamin B1). These vitamins are essential for a growing child, making them ideal to sneak into yummy breakfast wraps!

Makes 4 tortillas
Prep time: 5 minutes
Cooking time: 7–10 minutes

half a red pepper, diced
1 tsp olive oil
4 cherry tomatoes,
  quartered
3 eggs
5 tbsp milk
pinch of salt
1 tbsp grated Parmesan
  cheese
4 small flour tortillas,
  warmed

- Place the pepper into a large non-stick frying pan with the oil and sauté until tender.
- Add the tomatoes and cook for a 1–2 minutes.
- Whisk the eggs, milk and salt in a large bowl.
- Reduce the heat setting to medium and then add the egg mixture to the pan. Cook the mixture, stirring all the time until the eggs are scrambled and completely set.
- Spoon the vegetable mixture down the centre of each tortilla, sprinkle over some Parmesan and then roll up.
- Serve with Mumma's Homemade Tomato Ketchup (see page 47).

STRAWBERRY AND APRICOT SPREAD

Kids can't get enough of yummy spreadable treats. You can create a delicious fruit-flavoured cream cheese spread by stirring in fresh strawberries and chopped dried apricots. A tasty breakfast that's packed with nutrients and will also please the sweet-toothed members of the family!

Prep time: 10 minutes

115g full-fat cream cheese
60g strawberries, blended
50g dried apricots,
  chopped
1 tsp brown sugar

- Place the cream cheese, strawberries, apricots and sugar into a blender and blend for a few minutes.
- Scoop the mixture into a lidded container. The mixture can then be kept in the refrigerator for up to 3 days.
- Serve on toasted wholemeal bagels – a delicious kick-start to a busy day ahead!

Mum's Tip: *Don't forget to add the apricots. Apricots are a rich source of vitality-boosting vitamins, minerals and dietary fibre. Ideal to help support your child's energy levels throughout the day.*

BUBBLE AND SQUEAK PANCAKES ....

How sneaky is this lovely weekend breakfast treat? ('Broccoli for *breakfast*?' I hear you ask!) Broccoli is a premium 'superfood' that has many wonderful health benefits. Like oranges, broccoli is rich in vitamin C and beta-carotene. Broccoli also contains vitamins B1, B2, B3, B6, iron, magnesium, potassium, zinc and healthful amounts of fibre too.

Makes 6 pancakes
Prep time: 5 minutes
Cooking time: 30 minutes

400g potatoes
1 small head broccoli
1 tbsp rapeseed oil
3 spring onions, finely chopped
black pepper, to taste
100g grated cheese
1 tbsp grated Parmesan cheese
1 tsp mixed herbs
1 egg, beaten
2 tbsp flour

- Peel the potatoes, place in a pan of water and boil until soft.
- Divide the broccoli florets and steam for around 6 minutes.
- Heat a few drops of the oil in a frying pan. Add the spring onions and fry gently over a low heat until soft. Remove the pan from the heat.
- Drain and mash the potatoes. Place the potatoes and broccoli into a bowl and mix well.
- Stir in the spring onions, pepper, cheeses, herbs and egg. Add a little flour if the mixture becomes too 'wet'.
- Pour the oil into the pan, turn to medium heat.
- Fry spoonfuls of the mixture, turning once, for about 7 or 8 minutes, or until lightly browned.

Mum's Tip: Serve with some tasty sausages and a dollop of Mumma's Homemade Tomato Ketchup (see page 47).

GRANNY'S GRANOLA ···

Most shop-bought granola is loaded with sugar and other not-so-healthy ingredients. This homemade version contains less sugar and provides tastebud-tempting flavours and aromas such as vanilla and cinnamon.

Prep time: 5 minutes
Cooking time: 25 minutes

170g porridge oats
55g almonds, chopped
55g walnuts, chopped
55g coconut, shredded
55g sunflower seeds
55g pumpkin seeds
2 tbsp coconut oil
3 tbsp honey
1 tsp ground cinnamon
2 tsp vanilla extract
50g raisins
50g dried cranberries

- Preheat the oven to 180°C/Gas Mark 4. Combine the oats, nuts and seeds in a large bowl.
- In a saucepan, combine the coconut oil, honey, cinnamon and vanilla. Heat the mixture gently until the honey is just soft and everything is mixed well together. Remove from the heat, pour over the oaty mixture and combine well.
- Line a baking tray with baking paper and spread the granola over it. Bake for 20 minutes, checking every 5 minutes and moving around on the tray if necessary (to ensure it all browns evenly). When the granola is golden-brown, take out of the oven and allow to cool. Add raisins and cranberries. Serve with almond milk and, if not all eaten at once, store in an airtight container.

Mum's Tip: Adding sunflower seeds provides a great source of protein, which is essential for children's healthy growth and development.

SPINACH OMELETTE

Spinach is among the most nutritious foods you can give to your child. Spinach is an excellent source of iron, calcium, folic acid and vitamins A and C – all great for growing bones and brains.

Serves 2
Prep time: 5 minutes
Cooking time: 5–7 minutes

55g baby spinach
2 eggs
1 garlic clove, crushed
salt and pepper
1 tbsp milk
1 tbsp rapeseed oil
25g grated cheese
salt and pepper, to season

- Wash and steam spinach to pack's instructions and set aside. Break eggs into a bowl and whisk until they go frothy. Whisk in the garlic, salt and pepper and milk. Add in the spinach and stir.
- On a gentle heat, heat the non-stick pan. Add the rapeseed oil. Pour half the egg mixture into the middle of the pan. Cook for around 3 minutes on each side.
- Once cooked, sprinkle the omelette with cheese and season well. Fold omelette in half, allowing cheese to melt. Slide cooked omelette onto a serving plate, and season with salt and pepper to taste. Repeat with the remaining mixture.

Mum's Tip: Drink with a glass of orange juice as vitamin C really helps with absorbing iron.

3
SUPERB SNACKS

As a child, how many times did your parents tell you not to eat some delicious snack or treat because it would spoil your dinner? And, as a parent, how many times have you said the same thing to your children (even if you always said you never would)? The answer is: too many times to count. Right?

The thing is, snacks can actually be a rather important part of a child's daily diet and, if they are the right kind of food and given at the right times, they can boost levels of important nutrients within your child's body. This rebalances the body and reduces mood swings that can be caused by spikes in hunger and ups the child's energy levels so they are actually more active, despite eating more.

Snacks can help in the battle against obesity. Plus they are ideal for picky eaters who might not be so keen to try a proper home-cooked meal but will happily nibble on a well-thought-out snack. At least they will be eating something, and when it is wholesome and healthy parents can relax a little.

But remember, we're not talking chocolate chip cookies and cakes here. The snacks need to be healthy and nutritious and they need to be given at the right times too (that is, not just before a meal is about to be served!).

As well as what you are giving as a snack and the time you give it, portion size is something else to think about. You don't want your child's appetite to be completely reduced so that they don't eat their main scheduled meal and you want them to know when they're hungry. Children who graze on snacks all day often find it difficult to determine whether they actually need to eat or not (and usually they err on the side of caution and assume that they are hungry). As they grow, this problem can lead to weight issues and is a big cause of obesity in adults.

Structuring snacks is as important as structuring meals, so setting a schedule is an ideal way to go about ensuring that your children are able to work out for themselves what their hunger levels are. Give them food (including snacks) at the same time every day and the children themselves can choose how much they want to eat – and if they want to eat at all.

Bad habits when it comes to snack food are all too easy to fall into and they are incredibly difficult to get out of again. Giving sweets as a reward may seem harmless – even a good idea – but, in reality, it should be avoided. It can mean that children see sweets as being the ultimate food, better than anything else, because it is the reward. It's also not a good idea to give children sweets to 'keep them quiet' or pacify them. Fruit is a much better option or, if a meal is imminent, they will need to wait. It's good practice at being patient and they will eat more of their meal as well.

Establishing that snacks are available, but only at certain times, is a great way of showing children how to be responsible when it comes to food. It gives them a feeling of control which can help them to make good choices too.

The following are some great, nutritious ideas for snacks for your little ones.

SWEET VEGGIE FRITTATA

If you are looking for a healthy, nutritious, delicious dish that can hide a multitude of veggies, this simple-to-make frittata is for you. It's perfect for filling up empty stomachs after a long day at school.

Serves 6
Prep time: 5 minutes
Cooking time: 35 minutes

1 sweet potato, peeled and cubed into very small pieces
1 red onion, finely chopped
1 tbsp olive oil
1 garlic clove, crushed
1 green pepper, diced
small tin sweetcorn
salt and pepper
squeeze tomato purée
4 eggs
80g grated cheese

- Steam the sweet potato cubes for around 7 minutes. Gently fry the onion for a couple of minutes in a little oil, then add the garlic and cook for a further minute.
- Add the pepper and sweetcorn, season well and cook for a further 3–4 minutes. Add the tomato purée and sweet potatoes and combine well. Scoop into a round cooking dish and set aside.
- Crack the eggs into a bowl, add the cheese and whisk the mixture. Pour the mixture over the vegetables and stir. Place the pan in the centre of the oven and cook for 25 minutes.

Mum's Tip: *Rhymes can help your children when it comes to trying new food. It will make them laugh and they will be happier to give the unknown dish a try. An example could be: 'a filling veggie frittata, full of carrots and peas, this is a superhero lunch and it's so good for me!'*

HAPPY KALE CRISPS ....

Kale, like most green foods, is supremely healthy and nutritious. But, like most green foods, kids don't want to go anywhere near it. So creating kale crisps seems to be the best way to ensure the little ones gobble up their greens without even realising!

Serves 4
Prep time: 5 minutes
Cooking time: 10 minutes

half a bag of kale
3 tbsp coconut oil
1 tbsp honey
juice of half an organic lemon

- Wash the kale and trim the stems. Place the kale leaves into a large bowl.
- In a pan gently heat the oil. Then add the honey and lemon juice, simmer for a few minutes. Pour the mixture onto the kale leaves, then stir until they are well coated. Tip the coated leaves onto a baking tray and spread out in a single layer.
- Bake for 5 minutes, or until crisp but still green. Check often as they burn quickly. Leave to cool a little before serving.

Mum's Tip: Keep snack times relaxed and fun. I often engage my little boy, Max, in pretend play games before bringing a healthy snack to the table. For example, we might play a game of pirates where we need to stop for a snack of a 'Superpower Food' like kale crisps! The story might go something like this: 'Mighty Max needs to eat some superfoods to gain his magic powers and strength to beat the pirates and rescue Mickey the Marvellous Monkey.'

After playing, I always feel a sense of warmth come over me, as it feels good to spend time bonding through play as well as encouraging my little boy to eat something nourishing.

Sandwich Selections

Sandwiches can be a great snack for hungry bellies. You can cut them into different shapes using pastry cutters to make them more fun! They are also a great portable lunch; take them to the park for a picnic or pack in lunchboxes for school.

BANANA AND CINAMMON

Potassium-rich bananas can help boost children's energy and concentration skills.

Makes 2 sandwiches

1 banana
1 tsp butter
1 tsp honey
2 slices of brown bread
a pinch of cinnamon

- Cut the banana into thin slices. Spread butter and honey onto one slice of bread, place the banana slices on top and sprinkle with cinnamon. Place the other slice of bread on top and then cut into a sandwich.

Mum's Tip: Honey and cinnamon help support the immune system and defend the body from bacterial and viral attacks. A great treat to keep your little ones healthy!

EGG AND CRESS

Eggs are a complete protein food. Proteins provide building blocks to help your kids grow strong and healthy bodies.

Makes 2 sandwiches

1 free-range egg
½ tsp softened butter
2 slices brown bread
a pinch of cress

- Boil the egg for around 10 minutes, then drain and allow to cool in cold water. Spread the butter onto the bread. Peel the egg and mash it with a fork. Spread the mashed egg onto the bread, sprinkle with cress and place the other slice of bread on top. Cut into a sandwich.

Mum's Tip: I always like to use to use biscuit cutters in a variety of fun shapes such as stars or animals to make sandwiches look more appealing!

CREAM CHEESE AND APPLE

Apples are not only delicious, they also contain helpful amounts of soluble and insoluble fibre to keep your little one's digestive system running smoothly.

Makes 3 small finger sandwiches

1 tsp softened butter
2 slices wholemeal bread
1 small grated apple
25g Cheddar cheese

- Spread butter onto the bread then sprinkle the grated apple and cheese over one of the slices. Sandwich together and cut into small fingers.

Mum's Tip: *Mixing the apple and cheese together softens the crunch a little and makes the sandwich a little easier to eat.*

Yoghurt Pops

STRAWBERRY AND VANILLA YOGHURT POPS ....

Yoghurt pops made with fresh fruits make a nutritious, cool and tangy snack – especially delicious on warm, sunny days!

Makes 6 pops
Prep time: 5 minutes
Freezing time: 6 hours

1 tsp honey
200g chopped strawberries
12 tbsp vanilla yoghurt
6 lollipop moulds

- Pop the honey and strawberries into a blender and blend until smooth. Stir in the yoghurt before filling the lollipop moulds with the mixture and then freezing for 6 hours.
- You can also change pink pops to blue ones by using blueberries instead of strawberries. Yum!

Mum's Tip: Great to give hot, sweaty, thirsty kids at the end of a long school day!

FRUITY COOKIES

Apricots are a source of fibre and contain a range of vitamins and minerals that are essential to health.

Makes 12–15 cookies
Prep time: 30 minutes
Cooking time:
  15 minutes

160g butter
185g coconut sugar
  (or granulated sugar)
1 tbsp maple syrup
100g dried apricots,
  chopped
75g raisins
130g self-raising flour

- Preheat the oven to 180°C/Gas Mark 4.
- Cream together the butter and sugar in a large bowl until the mixture becomes light and fluffy. Add the maple syrup, apricots, raisins and sifted flour. Combine well.
- Roll the mixture into two logs, wrap in cling film and chill in the fridge for 20 minutes.
- Unwrap the roll, break off small balls and roll them into circles that are about 5cm wide and 0.5cm thick. Bake for 15 minutes until golden in colour.
- Cool on the tray for 5 minutes before transferring to a wire rack to cool completely.

Mum's Tip: This is a lovely cooking activity to do with the kids on a rainy day!

BRILLIANT BERRY DELIGHT

Cute little yoghurt and berry pots, perfect to give both you and your little one a much-needed midday energy boost!

Serves 4
Prep time: 5 minutes

12 ripe strawberries
12 blueberries
12 raspberries
4 pots of fromage frais

- Finely slice the strawberries and then combine them with the blueberries and raspberries. Divide between four lidded pots and place a dollop of fromage frais on top of each one. Place the lid on each pot and chill in the fridge until lunchtime.

RAINBOW FRUIT KEBABS

My kids love these fruit skewers, they are a colourful and fun way to get kids to eat fruit. They'll love helping to make them, too.

Makes 6 kebabs
Prep time: 5–10 minutes

6 blackberries
6 strawberries
6 tangerine segments
1 banana, sliced into 6 thick
  chunks
6 peeled pineapple chunks
6 peeled kiwi fruit slices
6 green grapes, deseeded
  and halved
12 blueberries

- Take 6 wooden skewers and then thread on one piece of each fruit, along with 2 blueberries at the end! Makes 6 healthy snacks – perfect for when your kids have friends over for play dates.

Energy Balls

Energy balls do exactly what you would expect them to with a name like that; this protein based snack is healthy and delicious, boosting energy levels for your little ones through the use of almonds and cranberries.

OATMEAL AND CRANBERRY ENERGY BALLS

Makes 17 balls
Prep time: 10 minutes
Cooling time: 30 minutes

50g oats
30g coconut, shredded
30g almonds, chopped
50g dried cranberries,
  chopped
1 tbsp honey
140g almond butter

- Mix all of the ingredients together in a bowl and, once the mixture is well combined, make 17 balls, about 2.5cm across.
- Place the balls on a tray lined with baking paper and pop in the fridge for about 30 minutes.

Mum's Tip: These balls can be a little sticky, so to avoid too much mess keep them in the fridge until you're ready to eat them.

AVOCADO AND CHOCOLATE CHIP ENERGY BALLS

Makes 17 balls
Prep time: 10 minutes
Cooling time: 30 minutes

85g oats
1 avocado (Make sure it's
  ripe. It needs to be pitted
  and mashed.)
1 tbsp brown sugar
1 tsp vanilla extract
100g peanut butter
1 tbsp chia seeds
5 tbsp chocolate chips

- Mix all the ingredients together in a bowl. Once the mixture is completely combined, make 17 little balls about 2.5cm wide.
- Place the balls on a tray lined with baking paper and pop in the fridge for half an hour or so.

COCONUT AND APRICOT ENERGY BALLS

Makes 17 balls
Prep time: 15 minutes
Cooling time: 30 minutes

**30g cashew nuts, chopped
50g oats
70g dried apricots,
  chopped
30g coconut, shredded
2 tsp vanilla extract
180g cashew butter**

- Preheat the oven to 200°C/Gas Mark 6 and roast the cashew nuts for 5 minutes. Once roasted, blend in a food processor.
- Mix all the remaining ingredients in a bowl and, once they are well combined, make 17 little balls, about 2.5cm wide.
- Place the balls on a tray lined with baking paper and pop in the fridge for 30 minutes.

BROCCOLI AND CHEESE MUFFINS

Savoury muffins always go down well with the little ones and they are ideal for packed lunches or park picnics.

Makes 12 muffins
Prep time: 10 minutes
Cooking time: 30 minutes

**1 small head of broccoli, cut
  into tiny florets
220g plain flour
1 tsp baking powder
150ml milk
2 medium eggs
140g grated cheese
2 tbsp rapeseed oil**

- Preheat oven to 180°C/Gas Mark 4. Steam the broccoli until tender (about 5 minutes). Whilst the broccoli is steaming, mix the flour, baking powder, milk, eggs and cheese together. When the broccoli is cooked, mash it with a fork and add that to the mixture too. Stir well.
- Spoon the mixture into a greased muffin tin and cook for around 30 minutes (or until golden). Allow to cool and enjoy!

Mum's Tip: These can be eaten cold or hot, but they are excellent when warm on cold days as they really keep little fingers cosy.

BANANA BREAD

There are always leftover bananas, no matter how many you buy – and children often won't even touch the ones that are turning brown. Luckily, those brown bananas are just the thing to put into this banana bread recipe.

Prep time: 15 minutes
Cooking time: 1 hour

4 ripe bananas
250g coconut sugar (or granulated sugar)
2 eggs
150g butter, softened
1 tsp cinnamon
250g self-raising flour
2 tsp baking powder
100g walnuts, chopped
100g raisins

- Preheat the oven to 190°C/Gas Mark 5. Grease and line a loaf tin with baking paper.
- Mash the bananas in a bowl, then add the sugar and combine. Add the eggs and use an electric whisk (if possible) to ensure everything is mixed well. Add the butter and cinnamon and whisk again for a few minutes.
- Sieve in the flour and baking powder and fold the mixture together before adding the chopped walnuts and raisins. Stir, then pour the mixture into the loaf tin and bake for 1 hour or until a knife comes out clean from the middle.
- Leave to cool and then remove the loaf. Serve in thick slices!

Mum's Tip: This cake can be stored in an airtight container for up to 3 days. It's perfect for a picnic.

TORTILLA PIZZAS

Makes 4
Prep time: 5 minutes
Cooking time: 12–15 minutes

**100g Mumma's Tomato
Ketchup (see p.47)**
4 small flour tortillas
50g mozzarella, shredded
**20 pieces of mini
pepperoni, optional**
50g grated cheese
10g fresh parsley
100g sweetcorn

• Preheat the oven to 200°C/Gas Mark 6.
• Spread the tomato sauce over the tortillas and layer with the mozzarella cheese and pepperoni, if required. Evenly spread the grated cheese over all 4 tortillas, then add the parsley and sweetcorn and cook for about 12 minutes.

Dipping

Dips make everything better. That's a fact. Give a child a plate of veg and they'll grimace. Give them a plate of veg and a bowl of delicious dip and the whole lot will be gone in minutes. A new study by the *Journal of the Academy of Nutrition and Dietetics* has proved this fact – one that parents have known for ever – and, perhaps surprisingly, it was discovered that the favourite dips were those containing herbs and spices.

SUNSET DELIGHT

Prep time: 5 minutes
Cooking time: 25 minutes

1 beetroot, quartered
1 small garlic clove, peeled
1 tbsp rapeseed oil
1 tsp grated Parmesan
1 tsp honey
3 tbsp cream cheese

- Preheat the oven to 200°C/Gas Mark 6.
- Put the beetroot quarters and garlic into a small roasting dish and cover with the oil. Roast for around 25–30 minutes until tender and allow to cool a little.
- Pop the beetroot, garlic and Parmesan into a food processor. Add the honey and cream cheese and blend.
- Serve with breadsticks or vegetables.

ROASTED CARROT DIP

Prep time: 5 minutes
Cooking time: 20 minutes

2 large carrots, roughly
chopped
2 garlic cloves, peeled
2 tbsp olive oil
salt and pepper to taste
3 tbsp cream cheese

- Preheat oven to 200°C/Gas Mark 6.
- Toss the carrots and garlic with the olive oil, salt and pepper and lay them on a baking sheet. Roast for about 20 minutes, until tender.
- When the carrots are cooked put them in a blender with the cream cheese and blend until smooth and creamy.
- This dip can be stored in an airtight container for up to 3 days.

HAPPY HUMMUS

Prep time: 5 minutes

400g tinned chickpeas
30g baby spinach
2 tbsp rapeseed oil
2 garlic cloves, crushed
the juice of half a lemon
1 tbsp water
2 tbsp cream cheese
½ tsp ground cumin
1 tsp paprika
sprinkle of salt to taste

- Rinse and drain the chickpeas and place onto a clean tea towel. Rub them hard to remove the skins. Pop the chickpeas into a food processor with the remaining ingredients and blend until smooth and creamy.
- This hummus can be stored in an airtight container for up to a week, and can be frozen for up to two months.

RED PEPPER DIP

Prep time: 5 minutes

1 jar of roasted red peppers,
  drained and chopped
1 tbsp fresh basil
1 garlic clove, crushed
1 tbsp cream cheese

- Blend the peppers, basil and garlic in a food processor. Add the cream cheese. Blend until smooth.

GORGEOUS GUACAMOLE

Prep time: 10 minutes

1 ripe avocado, skinned
   with the stone removed
½ small red onion, finely
   chopped
1 garlic clove, crushed
1 ripe tomato, finely
   chopped
2 tbsp lime juice
salt and pepper to season

- Mash the avocados in a medium bowl using a fork or potato masher. Next, throw in the onion, garlic, tomato and lime juice. Mix well and season to taste.

CARAMELISED ONION AND RICOTTA DIP

**Prep time: 5 minutes
Cooking time: 20 minutes**

1 large brown onion
1 tbsp rapeseed oil
1 tsp brown sugar
½ tsp honey
170g ricotta cheese
tomato purée

- Sauté the onion over a low heat for about 10–15 minutes. Make sure you stir them to prevent them from burning. When they are softened and turning golden, sprinkle the sugar over the top and stir well. Cook for a further 5 minutes before blending in a food processor. Add the honey and blend until smooth.
- In a separate bowl, mix the ricotta cheese with the purée, add the onion mixture and serve. The dip will last for a few days in the fridge.

Mum's Tip: *Making up fun rhymes will help encourage children to try new food. 'Dips are fun and dips are yum, dips are goodness in my tum! They grow strong bones, they keep me fit, I shall eat up every bit'!*

Nut Butters

Nut butters are a great alternative to standard butters, packed full of all the essential nutrients that growing children need to keep them fit and healthy. They are fantastic for spreading on oatcakes and bread but they can be used in everyday cooking too.

HOMEMADE PEANUT BUTTER

Prep time: 5 minutes
Cooking time: 15 minutes

250g raw peanuts
3 tbsp coconut oil
2 tsp honey
1 banana, chopped

- Preheat the oven to 180°C/Gas Mark 4.
- Spread the peanuts out on a baking tray in a single layer and pour the oil over the top. Roast the peanuts for about 15 minutes, remembering to turn every 5 minutes so that they are completely coated in the oil. This also stops them burning. Once cooked, take them out of the oven and leave them to cool.
- When they are cool, pop them into a blender with the honey and blend until smooth. Add the banana and blend for around a minute or so. Use the spread immediately or put into an airtight container and leave in the fridge for use within a few days.

Mum's Tip: This fabulously tasty peanut butter is perfect on a toasted wholewheat waffle topped with sliced banana and drizzled with honey . . . Yum! But remember, this one is only for children aged 12 months or older.

CASHEW NUT BUTTER

Prep time: 10 minutes
Cooking time: 5 minutes

240g cashew nuts

- Preheat the oven to 190°C/Gas Mark 5. Spread the cashew nuts over a baking tray and roast for about 5 minutes. Once cooked, pop the cashew nuts into a blender and blend on high speed for up to 10 minutes, until it's creamy. It will be necessary to scrape the mixture off the sides of the blender as you go.
- Place the butter into an airtight container and store in the fridge.

Mum's Tip: Cut an apple into wedges and dip them into the butter – the kids will love it!

SWEET ALMOND DIP

Prep time: 15 minutes

250g raw almonds
1 tsp honey

- Pop the nuts into a blender and blend on high speed for around 15 minutes, until the mixture is creamy. If you need to, use a spatula to remove the excess mixture from the sides of the blender in order to keep blending away! When the nuts are completely blended, add the honey and pulse again. Put the butter into an airtight container and keep in the fridge.

Mum's Tip: You need to be patient with this one, as the nuts can take a while to turn into a creamy mixture. It will happen though. You just need to wait for the oils to be released.

FRUIT DIPPERS

Fruit is a lot easier to get into kids than veg, but it is just as healthy. A fruit platter for a morning snack – especially with additional nut butter – will always go down well.

Prep time: 5 minutes

1 pineapple, peeled, cored and cut into chunks
1 red apples, cored and cut into 16 slices
2 tangerines, peeled and in segments

- Mix all the fruit pieces up together, place them in a bowl and put a tub of nut butter on the side. If the kids don't want to use their fingers (or you would prefer them not to), use cocktail sticks.

TASTE EXPLOSION

Due to their pretty looks, vegetable platters are a fabulous way to encourage less-adventurous eaters to give veggies a try!

Prep time: 10 minutes

1 carrot
2 sticks of celery
half a cucumber
1 red pepper
1 yellow pepper
1 small head of broccoli

- Cut up the veggies into strips (divide the broccoli into florets) and serve with a dip.

PITTA DIPPING CHIPS

Sometimes parents have to be sneaky to keep their kids healthy and this is one of those times. These 'chips' are a popular dish with the little ones, especially when they plunge them into a dip that's full of hidden veg!

Prep time: 5 minutes
Cooking time: 15 minutes

2 tbsp rapeseed oil
1 garlic clove, crushed
1 tsp onion salt
4 pitta breads, cut into 8
  single-layered triangles

• Preheat the oven to 200°C/Gas Mark 6. Mix the oil, garlic and onion salt in a small bowl and brush the mixture over the pitta bread pieces.
• Pop the pieces onto a baking tray and bake for 12–15 minutes until golden. They burn quickly!

Sauces

A great sauce can mean the difference between an average meal and a brilliant one. They really can make or break a meal. So it's handy to have some delicious sauce recipes on standby to jazz up dinner time.

MUMMA'S TOMATO KETCHUP

Prep time: 2 minutes
Cooking time: 10 minutes

1 tbsp rapeseed oil
150g cherry tomatoes
1 tsp brown sugar
1 tsp salt
1tsp red wine vinegar
½ tsp garlic powder
¼ tsp onion powder
¼ tsp paprika
3 tsp Worcestershire sauce
3 tsp tomato purée

- Heat all ingredients in a saucepan on a gentle heat for around 10 minutes, stirring occasionally. Cool.
- Pour carefully into a blender or food processor. Blend until smooth. Allow to cool and serve or, alternatively, store in an airtight container for around 2-3 weeks in the fridge.

LEMON MAYONNAISE

Prep time: 5 minutes

200g mayonnaise
1 tsp fresh lemon juice
1 tbsp parsley, chopped

- Mix all of the ingredients together and pop into an airtight container. Place in the fridge until you are ready to use it.

SWEET CHILLI SAUCE

Cooking time: 5 minutes

1 tbsp red wine vinegar
2 garlic cloves, crushed
2 tbsp honey
½ tsp chilli flakes
1 tsp tomato purée

- Put everything into a saucepan and bring to the boil. Once boiled, reduce the heat and allow to simmer for 2–3 minutes, or until the sauce starts to thicken.
- Once it has thickened, remove from the heat and allow to cool before serving.

Smoothies

Can there be anything better than a smoothie? Colourful and tasty like a fruity milkshake (and therefore irresistible), but packed full of vitamins and nutrients, this is one sure-fire way to get the little ones to have their five-a-day. Note: each recipe serves two people.

MORNING GLORY

Prep time: 5 minutes

1 apple, cored
1 handful of spinach
200ml coconut water
4 apricots, pitted (dried if
not in season)
2 tbsp probiotic vanilla
yoghurt

• Use a food processor to blend the apple, spinach and coconut water until smooth. Add the apricots and yoghurt and blend again.

MANGO MANIA

Prep time: 5 minutes

1 handful of kale
½ mango, peeled and
chopped
1 banana
200ml orange juice
1 tsp chia seeds

• Put the kale, mango, banana and orange juice into a blender and blend until smooth. Add the chia seeds and blend them again, making sure it is smooth.

COCONUT DREAM

Prep time: 5 minutes

1 handful of coconut flesh
1 handful of spinach
200ml coconut water
1 apple, cored
1 tbsp mint leaves

• Using a food processor, blend the coconut flesh, spinach and coconut water until smooth. Add the apple and mint leaves to the mix, and pulse again until really smooth.

FANTASTIC FLUSH

Prep time: 5 minutes

1 apple, cored
5 pieces of pineapple, cut
 into 2cm chunks
200ml cranberry juice

• Blend it all up until smooth!

STRAWBERRIES AND CREAM

Prep time: 5 minutes

100g strawberries
200ml milk
2 tbsp double cream

• Pop everything into a food processor and blend until completely smooth.

SUPER SMOOTHIE

Prep time: 5 minutes

1 banana
1 avocado
200ml almond milk
4 walnuts
1 tsp cinnamon

• Blend the banana, avocado and almond milk to a smooth consistency. Add the walnuts and cinnamon and blend again.

SUNSHINE SURPRISE

Prep time: 5 minutes

1 banana
1 carrot, grated
200ml orange juice
1 mandarin
2 tbsp Greek yoghurt

• Add the banana, carrot and orange juice to a blender and pulse until smooth. Add the mandarin and yoghurt and blend again.

GLORIOUS GREENS

Prep time: 5 minutes

1 avocado
1 handful of spinach
200ml of coconut water

• Blend all of the ingredients together until completely smooth.

Mum's Tip: *Get the kids involved. There is nothing the little ones enjoy more than helping Mum or Dad in the kitchen and it is useful for them to see how their food is prepared. As for smoothies, why not create your own? Your child can pick out the ingredients and blend them (under supervision) for a brand-new taste sensation!*

4
LOVELY LUNCHES

Breakfast is often called the most important meal of the day, but lunch should never be forgotten – a healthy lunch keeps children alert and focused for whatever the afternoon may bring. But being healthy on its own isn't going to entice your child's tastebuds; lunch needs to be tasty too or it won't get eaten.

Many children opt for a packed lunch at school and that means it's up to us as parents to ensure these are nutritious, delicious and inspiring. It's a tricky task; it can be hard coming up with different lunchtime ideas. This can mean ready-packaged snacks are used but, although these are convenient, they are full of saturated fat, salt and sugar and should be avoided.

Instead of using these, try to use as much natural produce as possible. Fruit and vegetables are great for growing bodies; they are high in fibre whilst being low in fat, salt and sugar – making them an ideal lunchtime snack.

TIPS TO PERSUADE YOUR CHILD TO EAT THEIR LUNCH

Get them involved

It may not be your favourite task, but planning and preparing their own lunchbox can be pretty exciting for children. Not only will they enjoy it, but when they're allowed to get involved, they will be more likely to try it. Basically, if they've had a hand in the preparation, they'll be more convinced when it comes to eating it.

Small portions

Children can sometimes have a hard time making a choice when it comes to what to eat. Rather than one big meal, it's more fun for them (and easier) to pack small things. Finger food is perfect – kids love the idea of eating with their hands.

Lunch Ideas

VEGGIE WRAP

Sandwiches are great and all, but a wrap is a fun and interesting way to jazz up an old favourite.

Wraps are ideal for lunchboxes. They can be prepared in advance, easily held, and enjoyed on the go. Plus, you can surprise children with the fillings as they're not so easy to see – hide your veggies inside and as long as the wrap tastes great, the kids won't be tempted to take a peek.

Makes 1
Prep time: 5 minutes

2 tsp cream cheese
1 small tortilla wrap
1 tbsp carrot, grated
2 slices of red pepper, finely
  sliced into matchsticks
3 baby spinach leaves

• Spread the cream cheese over the tortilla, then add the vegetables along one side. Roll up tight and tuck the ends in neatly.

STRAWBERRY SENSATION

No one is averse to the wonder that is the strawberry! This is the perfect summer wrap and it makes a change from the savoury ones that are the norm.

Makes 1
Prep time: 5 minutes

1 tsp double cream
1 tsp cream cheese
1 small tortilla
2 strawberries, quartered
pinch of coconut sugar (or
  granulated sugar)

• Mix the cream and the cream cheese together and spread the mixture onto the tortilla. Add the strawberries along one side, sprinkle a pinch of coconut sugar over the top before rolling the wrap up tightly and ensuring the ends are tucked in neatly.

CHICKEN WRAP

My kids never used to like these wraps until they had a go at assembling them themselves. They love getting involved in making their own food. Even my fussiest eater loves these now!

Makes 1
Prep time: 5 minutes

1 tsp cream cheese
1 small tortilla
3 baby spinach leaves
2 strips of chicken, using
  leftover chicken from a
  roast is ideal for this
sprinkle of paprika

- Spread the cream cheese onto the wrap and place the spinach and chicken on top. Sprinkle the paprika over and tuck everything in tightly.

FRUITY DELIGHT

Good looks and good taste – these gorgeous wraps are beautiful and delicious; who could ask for more? The fruits I've listed below are just an idea – you can use your kid's favourites, but try to keep to the same colours as below to create a rainbow effect.

Makes 1
Prep time: 5 minutes

1 tsp honey
1 small tortilla
2 raspberries, halved
2 blueberries
8 green grapes, deseeded
  and quartered
1 strawberry, quartered

- Spread the honey on the tortilla and add the fruit before rolling the wrap tight and tucking the ends in neatly.

Sushi Sandwiches

Another twist on the traditional sandwich idea, these creative, healthy rolls are a fabulous way to get the children to eat their lunch, fuss-free. They might even try some different fillings!

BANANA RAMA

Prep time: 5 minutes

1 small banana
1 slice of bread
1 tsp peanut butter
sprinkle of cinnamon

- Cut the crusts off the slice of bread and lay it on a chopping board. Roll the bread flat with a rolling pin – it needs to be completely flat.
- Spread the peanut butter over the bread and then place the sliced banana at one end. Cut the banana to fit the bread.
- Sprinkle the banana with cinnamon and roll the bread over to make a wrap. Seal the join by pressing lightly.
- Cut into 4 pieces and serve.

Mum's Tip: *I would recommend eating these straightaway rather than putting in lunchboxes because the banana can start to brown and may put kids off.*

VEGGIE SLAW

Prep time: 5 minutes

1 slice of bread
1 tbsp cream cheese
1 tbsp red pepper, cut into matchsticks
1 tbsp yellow pepper, cut into matchsticks

- Cut the crusts off the bread and lay it on a chopping board. Use a rolling pin to squash it down until it is completely flat.
- Spread the cream cheese on the bread.
- Place the peppers at one end of the bread and roll the slice up into a wrap. Press lightly to seal, and cut into 4 pieces.

STUFFED PIZZA BALLS

A different take on the classic pizza! Kids will go crazy over a mealtime favourite and parents will love that there are hidden veggies inside.

Makes 12 balls
Prep time: 10 minutes
Cooking time: 20 minutes

100g red peppers, cut into matchsticks
100g yellow peppers, cut into matchsticks
1 small red onion, finely diced
1 tbsp rapeseed oil
1 clove of garlic, crushed
1 tsp ground mixed spice
100g grated Cheddar cheese
100g grated Parmesan
200g pizza dough

- Preheat the oven to 200ºC/Gas Mark 6. Line a baking tray with greaseproof paper.
- Fry the peppers and onion in the oil for about 2 minutes. Then add the garlic and spice and fry for another minute. Remove and set aside.
- Mix the cheeses together in a bowl and set aside.
- On a floured surface, roll out the dough into a large rectangle, then cut it into 12 equal squares. Top each square with some of the veg and some of the cheese. Pick up each side of the square of dough and seal before rolling into a ball. Be gentle!
- Place the pizza balls on the baking tray and brush with some more oil and a sprinkling of Parmesan. Bake for 15 to 20 minutes, until golden-brown.
- Serve immediately, or have cold in a lunchbox.

VEGGIE PATTIES

Veggie burgers are an ideal way to sneak veg into children's meals. Burgers are always a great hit with kids. Plus, done right, the kids will barely bat an eyelid about the lack of meat in their meal.

Makes 4 patties
Prep time: 10 minutes
Cooking time: 15 minutes

1 tsp rapeseed oil
1 small onion, diced
1 medium potato, grated
¼ head of broccoli, divided into small florets
1 medium carrot, grated
1 garlic clove, crushed
100g self-raising flour
1 tbsp milk
2 eggs, beaten
100g sweetcorn
100g Cheddar cheese
50g grated Parmesan

- Gently heat the oil in a pan and fry the onion, potato, broccoli and carrot for about 3 minutes. Add the garlic and sweetcorn and fry for another minute. Set aside.
- Mix the flour in a bowl with the milk and eggs. Add the potato and veg mixture as well as the cheeses and stir to make sure it's all combined.
- Heat a non-stick frying pan on a medium heat and add 1 heaped tbsp of the mixture to the pan. Cook for a couple of minutes on each side, and repeat with the rest of the mixture to make 4 patties. Serve warm.

LUNCH KABOBS

There is just something about having food on a stick that makes kids really want to eat it. Well, that's just fine with me because 'food on a stick' (otherwise known as kabobs) can be as varied and healthy as anything else!

Makes 2 kabobs
Prep time: 5 minutes

2 slices of wafer-thin ham
4 cubes of red Leicester cheese
4 chunks of pineapple
4 small cherry tomatoes

- Cut the slices of ham in half and fold each half twice, so that it is a cube (or as close to a cube as a piece of ham can get!).
- Thread a cube of cheese onto a kebab skewer, then the pineapple, then a cube of ham and then a tomato. Repeat, then do the same on a second skewer.
- Serve immediately or place into an airtight container for later.

RAINBOW COUSCOUS

Full of an array of colours, this dish not only looks delicious, it tastes great too.

Serves 4
Prep time: 5 minutes
Cooking time: 20 minutes

1 tbsp olive oil
1 red onion, diced
1 clove of garlic, crushed
1 red pepper, diced
2 carrots, grated
500ml vegetable stock
200g couscous
a handful of raisins
250g tinned sweetcorn

- Heat the oil in a medium-sized pan and add the onion, garlic, pepper and carrots. Gently fry for around 6–8 minutes, stirring occasionally.
- Pour in the vegetable stock and add the couscous. Stir well and allow to simmer for 10 minutes.
- When the couscous is nearly cooked, add the raisins and sweetcorn. Stir and fluff up the couscous with a fork.
- Serve immediately.

THREE-CHEESE PASTA

One of the best parts of this dish is the buttery crumb topping. I like the toasty crunch in contrast to the soft pasta shells. It gives pasta a different twist for a lunchtime snack.

Serves 2
Prep time: 5 minutes
Cooking time: 15 minutes

100g baby pasta, I use animal-shaped pasta
¼ head broccoli, divided into florets
100g frozen sweetcorn
1 tsp butter
1 clove of garlic, crushed
50g breadcrumbs
1 tsp grated Parmesan
50g Cheddar cheese, grated
2 tbsp ricotta cheese

- Cook the pasta to the pack instructions. Whilst it's cooking, steam the broccoli for 5 minutes, adding the sweetcorn to it after three minutes. When it is ready, set aside.
- In a pan over medium heat, cook the butter and garlic. Stir and cook for about 2 minutes, then add the breadcrumbs, Cheddar and Parmesan. Season well. Stir and remove from the heat.
- When the pasta is cooked, mix in the ricotta cheese and vegetables. Place in a small ovenproof dish and layer the breadcrumbs on top.
- Place under the grill until golden.
- Serve immediately.

CARROT CAKE SLICES

This is a great carrot cake recipe that will leave your kids wanting more!

Makes 8-10 slices
Prep time: 5 minutes
Cooking time: 30 minutes

200g butter
275g coconut sugar (or granulated sugar)
1 tsp vanilla extract
2 large eggs
180g self-raising flour
200g carrot, grated
1 tsp cinnamon

- Preheat the oven to 190°C/Gas Mark 5.
- Line a medium-sized baking tray with greaseproof paper.
- Gently melt the butter in a pan. When melted, remove from the heat and add the sugar, vanilla extract and eggs. Mix well.
- Mix the flour, carrot and cinnamon together in a bowl and add the butter mixture. Stir well.
- Spread the mixture onto the baking tray and bake for around 30 minutes, or until golden.
- Allow to cool before cutting into squares.

FRUITY MIX

This great recipe makes fruit more exciting. Kids love variety as well as colour and this fruit mix not only looks attractive but it tastes great too.

Makes 4 pots
Prep time: 10 minutes

1 apple, cored
1 firm mango
8 strawberries
8 blueberries
8 blackberries
chocolate sprinkles

- Cut the apple and mango into small pieces. Quarter the strawberries. Place all the fruit into a bowl and toss with chocolate sprinkles.
- Can be served in bowls or little tubs or stored in airtight containers and used for lunchboxes.

CASHEW AND CHOCOLATE ENERGY BARS

Delicately sweet yet crunchy and delicious, the fabulous cashew nut is packed with energy, antioxidants, minerals and vitamins that are essential for robust health.

Makes 8 bars
Prep time: 10 minutes
Cooking time: 20 minutes

7 tbsp honey
2 tbsp plain flour
2 tbsp coconut sugar (or granulated sugar)
2 tbsp cashew nut butter
50g chopped cashew nuts
50g sunflower seeds
50g oats
50g shredded coconut
50g chocolate chips

- Preheat the oven to 190°C/Gas Mark 5.
- Line a medium baking tray with greaseproof paper.
- In a large bowl, add the honey, flour, sugar and cashew nut butter. Mix well to combine.
- On a chopping board, roughly chop the cashew nuts and add them to the mixture. Then add the sunflower seeds, oats and shredded coconut. Mix together before folding in the chocolate chips.
- Place the mixture onto the baking tray, pressing the top of the mixture firmly to pack in the ingredients so it holds together well.
- Bake for around 20 minutes, then remove from the oven and allow to completely cool before slicing into 8 pieces.

Milkshakes

Banana, strawberry and even mango milkshakes are a great way to get more fruit into your child's diet in a way that they won't mind at all! Milkshakes are great for a delicious snack or to accompany a lunchtime meal.

BRILLIANT BANANA MILKSHAKE

Makes 1
Prep time: 10 minutes

250ml full-fat milk
1 banana
1 tsp vanilla extract

- Blend all the ingredients together in a blender and serve!

STRAWBERRIES AND CREAM MILKSHAKE

Makes 1
Prep time: 5 minutes

250ml full-fat milk
3 tbsp double cream
4 strawberries

- Pop all the ingredients into a blender, blend them up and serve.

MANGO MANIA MILKSHAKE

Makes 1
Prep time: 5 minutes

250ml full-fat milk
2 tbsp double cream
¼ mango
2 strawberries

- Put everything into a blender, whizz it up and enjoy!

5
DEVIOUS DINNERS

The idea of the entire family eating around the table together is a lovely one, but we all know it doesn't happen as often as we'd like, even if we're reluctant to admit it. We have such hectic lives, it's true, and it's so hard to squeeze everything in. All of us want to spend more quality time with our family but often can't find enough hours in the day.

Dinner is a time to relax, recharge, laugh, tell stories and catch up on the day's ups and downs while developing a sense of who we are as a family. Over the past fifteen years researchers have confirmed what parents have known for a long time: sharing a family meal is good for the spirit, the brain and the health of all family members. Studies also indicate that dinner conversation is a more potent vocabulary-booster than reading and the stories told around the dinner table can help our children build resilience.

But the great thing about a shared mealtime is that the family togetherness can actually begin before the food is even ready. Cooking is a fun and practical way to reconnect as a family. Whether it is making family recipes or creating new ones, these moments in the kitchen will make powerful memories that your children will love. Plus, for those children who are, shall we say, more fussy when it comes to trying new things, if they've helped to make it themselves then they should be more inclined to eat it.

It is important to eat together as a family, but if that isn't possible every day of the week then maybe start with weekends? Make those nights special, make them cherished. And gradually build up to more in the week if you can.

Once you have the food on the table, it can be tricky to keep everyone interested – teenagers and toddlers are just as easily distracted as one another. But there are some ways to keep their attention for long enough to have a conversation and ensure they get something to eat!

DINNERTIME GAMES AND ACTIVITIES FOR YOUNGER CHILDREN

Pretend: One great way to keep the younger ones entertained around dinnertime is to pretend that the kitchen (and dining room if you have one) is their restaurant. They are the chefs and they need to take your order, prepare your food and serve it. They can even be instrumental in thinking up the menu in the first place. Of course, they may need help, but this is where the togetherness comes in.

Guessing games: The 'Can You Remember?' game is a great one to play around the dinner table because there is always something to see. Get them to close their eyes and ask a question such as, 'How many glasses on the table?' See if they can remember! Or what about a game of 'guess the ingredients', assuming they didn't help you cook, of course . . . And then there is the old favourite, I Spy.

DINNERTIME GAMES AND ACTIVITIES FOR OLDER CHILDREN

There are so many games that can be played with older children around the dinner table, making this family time one to really look forward to every time it happens. Whether it is every night or every now and then, these games will make it something special.

- Guess the emotion: each family member takes a turn at pulling a face that is meant to describe an emotion . . . and the others have to guess what it is.
- Story time: this has many variations, but one particularly fun version is where each person around the table adds to the story by making up the next sentence.
- Would you rather? This really is as simple as it sounds! Ask a question with two options and see what your family would choose. Bonus points if the others predict correctly!
- Joke of the day: everyone has to tell a joke. The one that gets the biggest laugh is the winner.
- Believe it or not: everyone around the table has to tell three incredible stories. One of them will be true, but it's up to the rest of the family to choose which one.
- My great wish: take turns talking about your greatest wish and the plans you are hatching to get there. What a fantastic way to find out more about your children's goals and ideas and it's also a lovely way for them to find out more about you.

- I've never: everyone has to name one thing they have never done, but that they think everyone else around the table has. They keep going until they get it wrong and discover someone else who hasn't done it either.

Now you have an idea of how to get the children involved and keep them occupied at dinnertime, here are some fabulous recipes for devious dinners that they will love!

COWBOY CASSEROLE

Cowboy Casserole is a tasty dish containing sausages that kids absolutely adore – as do the adults. This is the perfect dish for a cold winter's day and since it includes a ton of hidden veg and some sneaky aduki beans (which contribute to growth, repair and increase energy), it's a pretty healthy bonanza too!

Serves 4
Prep time: 15 minutes
Cooking time: 20 minutes

1 tbsp rapeseed oil
1 brown onion, finely sliced
2 garlic cloves, crushed
2 celery stalks, finely sliced
2 small carrots, grated
1 red pepper, diced
100ml vegetable stock
6 pork sausages
400g tinned tomatoes
1 tbsp dried basil
1 can aduki beans (380g)
parsley, to serve

- Heat the oil in a pan on a medium heat. Add the onion and cook gently for 3 minutes. Then add the garlic, celery, carrot and peppers and cook for a further 3 minutes to make a purée.
- Place in a food processor with the vegetable stock and purée. Set aside.
- Add the sausages to the pan and cook to pack instructions. When the sausages are cooked, cut them into 1cm slices and place back in the pan.
- Add the purée to the sausages and mix so that everything is covered. Add the beans and cook for a further 4–5 minutes.
- Garnish with parsley and serve with Cauliflower Mash (see page 91).

Mum's Tip: This is a great meal to serve around the campfire, telling stories to little campers. I usually make up the purée before we go camping and add it to the sausages once cooked.

CRAFTY CARBONARA

Spaghetti is always fun (if a little messy!) and it's a bonus that this particular recipe is delicious and healthy too! There's a sneaky courgette in this recipe, so the whole dish ends up being packed with vitamin K, vitamin C, potassium and dietary fibre.

Serves 4
Prep time: 5 minutes
Cooking time: 15 minutes

300g spaghetti
1 tbsp rapeseed oil
1 leek, finely sliced
1 courgette, finely sliced
2 cloves garlic
50g Parmesan, finely
  grated, plus extra to serve
1 egg
75ml double cream
4 tbsp cream cheese
6 slices of bacon, roughly
  chopped

- Boil a pan of water and cook the spaghetti according to the pack instructions.
- Add the oil to a frying pan. Gently fry the leek for 2 minutes. Add the courgette and fry for a further 2 minutes. Then add the garlic and fry for a further minute. Once cooked place the mixture into a food processor and blend with the Parmesan, egg, double cream and cream cheese until smooth. Set aside.
- In the same pan, fry the bacon for around 2 minutes on each side. Once cooked, roughly chop the bacon into small pieces.
- When the pasta is cooked, add it to the pan with the cut-up bacon, then quickly pour in the sneaky veg mixture. Using tongs or a long fork, lift up the spaghetti so it mixes easily. You want the mixture to thicken, but not scramble.
- Serve immediately with a little Parmesan and a pinch of black pepper.

BRILLIANT BEAN BURGERS

Not quite a hamburger, although they look enough like one that the kids probably won't mind giving them a go! Filling, packed with fibre and protein, these yummy burgers are a powerhouse of a meal.

Makes 6 large burgers
  or 10 small ones
Prep time: 10 minutes
Cooking time: 15 minutes

50g cashew nuts
3 tbsp rapeseed oil
150g finely chopped
  mushrooms
1 medium sweet potato,
  grated
3 spring onions, finely
  chopped
2 cloves of garlic, crushed
400g tinned kidney beans
1 tbsp mixed herbs
freshly ground black pepper
pinch of salt
1 egg
90g breadcrumbs
50g crushed almonds

- Place the cashew nuts in a food processor and pulse to a fine consistency. Set to one side.
- Place the oil in a frying pan and fry the mushrooms, sweet potatoes and spring onions. Cook for around 5–6 minutes, then add the crushed garlic and cook for a further minute.
- Meanwhile place the kidney beans in a bowl and mash with a potato masher. Then add the sautéed vegetables, mixed herbs and blended cashew nuts. Season well. Add the egg and mix all the ingredients together well.
- Roll the mixture into 6 burger-sized balls (or 10 smaller bite-sized balls). Flatten the balls slightly. Combine the breadcrumbs with the almonds and coat the burgers in the breadcrumb mixture.
- Add a little more oil to the frying pan and fry burgers for 3–4 minutes each side (Smaller sized burgers for 2–3 minutes).
- Serve in a burger bun with salad.

SEE-IN-THE-DARK CHICKEN

With a name like this, kids are going to be clamouring for a taste! Carrots have antibacterial and antiseptic properties, so getting your child to eat carrots will help boost their immunity. Also, carrots are an excellent source of vitamin C, which triggers the activity and functioning of the white blood cells which boost a child's health.

Serves 4
Prep time: 10 minutes
Cooking time: 35 minutes

2 tbsp rapeseed oil
2 chicken breasts, cut into 1cm chunks
1 onion, sliced finely
2 cloves of garlic, crushed
2 large carrots
1 medium sweet potato
300ml coconut milk
100g peas
3 tbsp vegetable stock, if needed
salt and pepper
coriander, to serve

- Add the oil to a medium pan and brown the chicken. Remove and set aside.
- Add a little more oil, then pop the onions into the pan. Fry for 2 minutes, then add the garlic and fry for a further minute.
- Chop up the carrot and sweet potato and add to the pan. Pour in the coconut milk and let simmer for 15 minutes. Once cooked, pour the mix carefully into a blender and blend until smooth.
- Place the chicken and the veg mixture back into the pan and simmer for around 5 minutes, then add the peas and simmer for a further 5 minutes. If the mixture starts to dry out, add some vegetable stock.
- Season, add a little coriander and serve with (preferably brown) fluffy rice.

CHEESY MEATBALLS

Parents love the fact that meatballs are so versatile and kids love the fact that they are so tasty. Plus, with hidden veg in them they can be the ideal dish to serve any night of the week.

Makes 8 meatballs
Prep time: 15 minutes
Cooking time: 35 minutes

(meatballs)
1 tbsp rapeseed oil
1 onion, chopped finely
1 medium carrot, grated
2 cloves of garlic
1 medium egg
250g minced beef
2 tsp spicy Italian herb mix
1 tbsp grated Parmesan
salt and pepper
70g white breadcrumbs
8 small mozzarella balls
Parmesan

(sauce)
1 tbsp rapeseed oil
1 brown onion, chopped
2 cloves of garlic
1 carrot, grated
400g tinned chopped tomatoes
1 tsp Worcestershire Sauce
1 tbsp mixed herbs
1 bunch of basil
salt and pepper
8 tbsp beef stock

- Sauté the onion and carrot for around 3 minutes before adding the garlic and cooking for a further minute. Remove the carrot and the garlic mix from the frying pan and place into a bowl. Beat in the egg, then add the minced beef, spices, and Parmesan. Season. Add the breadcrumbs and knead the ingredients together by hand.
- Shape the meat mixture into 8 large balls. Make an indentation in the centre of each ball with your thumb and stuff a mozzarella ball inside. Mould the meat back around the cheese. Brown in a frying pan and set aside on kitchen roll to soak up any additional oil.
- Meanwhile, make the sauce. Heat the oil in a saucepan and gently cook the onion until soft. Add the garlic and carrots and cook for a few more minutes.
- Add the tin of tomatoes, Worcestershire sauce and mixed herbs. Then add the basil, torn, and browned meatballs. Season with salt and pepper and leave to simmer for 30 minutes, adding stock every 10 minutes or so to stop the mixture from drying out.

Mum's Tip: Serve this meal with spiralized courgettes instead of spaghetti. Courgettes are high in water and help detox your body, ridding it of unwanted toxins and leaving you and your child refreshed and hydrated. Courgettes have an abundance of dietary fibre, which helps keep us fuller for longer and assists with everyday digestion.

SWEET SHEPHERD'S PIE

What is the world's healthiest food that is also a great source of vitamin A, vitamin C, manganese, copper, pantothenic acid and vitamin B6? It's the sweet potato, which this recipe has in abundance. Not only that, but it freezes well and reheats nicely, so you can prepare it in advance for when the schedule is extra busy.

Serves 4–6
Prep time: 15 minutes
Cooking time: 50 minutes

1 tbsp rapeseed oil
1 large onion, sliced
2 medium carrots, grated
2 garlic cloves, crushed
500g lamb mince
2 tbsp tomato purée
1 heaped tsp Marmite
1 tbsp Worcestershire sauce
270ml beef stock
100g frozen peas
900g sweet potatoes, peeled and cut into chunks
1 tsp cornflour, if needed
50g grated cheese

• Heat the oven to 180°C/Gas Mark 4. Then heat the oil and sauté the onion and carrots for a few minutes before adding the garlic and cooking for a further minute. Add mince and brown, tipping away any excess fat. Add the tomato purée, Marmite and Worcestershire sauce and stir.
• Pour the stock over the mixture, add the peas and simmer for around 20 minutes.
• Meanwhile, steam the sweet potatoes for around 20 minutes (or until tender) and then mash.
• If the mixture is a little watery, mix up the cornflour with a little water and add to the mince mixture. This will help it to thicken.
• Place the mince into an ovenproof dish, tip the mash on top and ruffle with a fork. Bake for around 15 minutes before removing from the oven and sprinkling with cheese.
• Pop back into the oven and bake for a further 10–15 minutes. Serve immediately with the veg of your choice.

CHICKEN AND VEGETABLE PASTA BAKE

Not only is this dish easy to cook, but it's delicious too – there will be no complaints about the veggies inside it!

Serves 4–6
Prep time: 20 minutes
Cooking time: 35 minutes

(pasta)
1 courgette, thinly sliced
1 aubergine, quartered and thinly sliced
1 red pepper, thinly sliced
1 green pepper, thinly sliced
200g penne pasta
3 tbsp rapeseed oil
2 chicken breasts, skin removed, cut into 1cm pieces
150g Cheddar cheese, grated
20g grated Parmesan cheese, to serve

(sauce)
1 tbsp rapeseed oil
1 brown onion, sliced
1 carrot, grated
3 garlic cloves, crushed
1 tin of chopped tomatoes
1 tbsp Worcestershire sauce
75 ml chicken stock
1 tbsp basil leaves, torn
salt and pepper

- Preheat the oven to 200°C/Gas Mark 6. Place the vegetables for the pasta in an ovenproof dish with a little rapeseed oil and toss around, making sure all the vegetables are covered. Place in the centre of the oven for around 15 minutes, tossing the vegetables every 5 minutes. Whilst the veg is roasting, cook the pasta according to the pack instructions.
- For the sauce, heat the oil in a saucepan and gently sauté the onion until soft. Add the carrot and garlic and cook for a few more minutes. Add the tin of tomatoes, Worcestershire sauce and stock. Stir in the basil and season. Leave to simmer for 5 minutes. Remove the pan from the heat, cool slightly and carefully place in a food processor. Blend and set aside.
- Heat the oil in a frying pan and lightly brown the chicken. When the vegetables and pasta are ready, mix the chicken with the pasta and the sauce and pop in an ovenproof dish. Add the cheese and mix well.
- Bake for 15–20 minutes until the cheese is brown. Serve with Parmesan cheese for sprinkling.

Mum's Tip: I often serve this with a side salad to get my kids used to eating vegetables on their own.

HIDDEN VEGGIE QUICHE

This is my great-gran's recipe and we absolutely love it in my house. It's full of spring flavours and is packed full of vitamins and vegetables. It can be served with steamed vegetables in the winter or a salad in the summer. So versatile!

Serves 4-6
Prep time: 10 minutes
Cooking time: 55 minutes

1 small courgette, finely chopped
1 small yellow pepper, diced
1 small red pepper, diced
1 small red onion, finely chopped
1 tbsp rapeseed oil
2 whole cloves of garlic, peeled
6 slices of bacon, diced and the fat removed
4 large eggs
50ml milk
5 tbsp flour
75g grated Cheddar cheese
shortcrust pastry sheet

- Preheat the oven to 180°C/Gas Mark 4. Place the chopped-up vegetables into an ovenproof dish with the garlic cloves, add a little oil and roast for around 15 minutes.
- In the meantime, gently fry the bacon and set aside. When the vegetables are ready, place them in a food processor with the eggs, milk, flour and cheese. Mix on high speed until the mixture is smooth. Then gently stir in the diced bacon.
- Line an ovenproof dish with your pastry – ideally it should be a 20–25cm round ceramic flan dish. Leave some pastry hanging over the edge as this helps to prevent shrinkage and can be cut off once it is cooked.
- Pour the mixture into the pastry case and cook in the centre of the oven for around 30–40 minutes. Serve warm or cold.

Mum's Tip: I often pop a slice of this quiche in my children's lunchbox instead of a sandwich. It makes a change and it's nice and healthy.

FABULOUS FISH PIE

Fish is an excellent source of vitamin B and with the added bonus of the sneaky veg in the topping, this is an all-round stellar dish.

Serves 4-6
Prep time: 15 minutes
Cooking time: 1 hour

600g potatoes, peeled and halved
400g sweet potatoes, peeled and cut into chunks
3 tbsp double cream
25g butter
1 small leek, finely chopped
25g plain flour
400ml milk
1 tbsp thyme
75g cheese, grated
1 pack of fish pie mix, around 500g of cod, salmon, smoked haddock etc.

- Preheat the oven to 180°C/Gas Mark 4. Cook the potatoes in boiling water until tender (around 25 minutes). At the same time, steam the sweet potatoes for around 10 minutes. Drain and set aside. When the potatoes are cooked, drain them and add the sweet potatoes and the double cream. Mash and set aside.
- Place the butter into a saucepan and gently melt it on a medium heat. Then add in the leek and fry for around 3-4 minutes. Gently sieve in the flour whilst stirring continuously. Slowly whisk in the milk, a little at a time (a balloon whisk is ideal). Bring the mixture to the boil and stir to remove all lumps. Cook for another 5-7 minutes to allow it to thicken. Once thickened, add the thyme and cheese and allow to melt. Stir the fish into the sauce before placing it in an ovenproof dish.
- Smooth the mash over the top, forking the surface. Bake for around 35 minutes until the potato is nice and golden.

MARVELLOUS MUSHROOM RISOTTO ....

Despite its notoriety as a tricky dish to master, risotto – or at least this version of it – isn't really that hard. Plus it's all cooked in one dish, so preparation (and clearing up) is super easy! Kids love risotto and it's incredibly easy to hide veg in it, too.

Serves 4–6
Prep time: 10 minutes
Cooking time: 30 minutes

1 tbsp rapeseed oil
1 large onion, chopped
200g mushrooms, sliced
2 cloves garlic, crushed
240g risotto rice
500ml chicken stock
80g Parmesan, grated
15g parsley, chopped
salt and pepper to taste

- In a medium-sized saucepan, heat the oil and add the onion, mushrooms and garlic. Cook for around 2–3 minutes.
- Pour in the risotto rice and then gradually add the stock. Stir occasionally until rice is tender (20–25 minutes).
- Remove from the heat and stir in the Parmesan and parsley. Season. Serve immediately.

LOVELY LASAGNE ....

This version of the classic Italian dish can be made ahead of time and kept in the freezer, ready to go. Eat it with a fresh salad or some homemade garlic bread.

Serves 4–6
Prep time: 20 minutes
Cooking time: 1 hour

2 chicken breasts, cut into thin strips
1 tbsp mixed herbs
200g butternut squash, diced
1 tbsp rapeseed oil
100g baby spinach
6-8 lasagne sheets
salt and pepper

(red sauce)
2 tbsp rapeseed oil
2 red peppers, cut into chunks
400g tinned tomatoes with herbs
1 tbsp Worcestershire sauce
3 cloves of garlic, crushed
1 bunch of basil, torn

(white sauce)
25g butter
600ml whole milk
25g plain flour
380g tinned butter beans, drained
120g cheese
salt and pepper

- Preheat the oven to 190°C, drizzle the peppers for the red sauce in oil and roast for around 15 minutes. Season the chicken strips with the mixed herbs.
- Whilst the peppers are cooking, steam the butternut squash for around 20 minutes. Sauté the chicken in a frying pan with 1 tbsp of rapeseed oil until browned. Once the chicken and the squash are done, combine and set aside.
- Once the peppers are cooked, place in a food processor with the tomatoes, Worcestershire sauce, garlic and basil. Blend until smooth then set aside.
- Next, make the white sauce. Place butter, milk and flour in the saucepan over a low heat and whisk continuously. Once the sauce has thickened, take off heat, add 100g of cheese and allow to melt. Carefully pour into a food processor and blend with the butter beans.
- In an ovenproof dish, place some of the red sauce at the bottom of the dish to form a layer. Add a layer of the chicken and butternut squash mixture, followed by a layer of spinach. Layer the white sauce over the top and then two or three pasta sheets. Repeat until all the ingredients are used. Finish with a pasta layer and top with the white sauce. Sprinkle with leftover cheese to cover the top and cook for around 40 minutes.

Mum's Tip: Get the kids to help make some homemade garlic bread (see page 76) for this dish. It's a great way to bond in the kitchen and encourages them to tuck in.

GORGEOUS GARLIC BREAD

Garlic bread is a winner with my kids! They love helping to make it as much as they enjoy eating it.

Prep time: 5 minutes
Cooking time: 15 minutes

**1 medium baguette/
French stick
5 cloves garlic, crushed
80g butter**

- Preheat the oven to 180°C/Gas Mark 4. Slice the baguette equally into 3cm pieces (be careful not to slice right though).
- Mix the garlic up with the butter. Divide the mixture equally between the slices of bread.
- Wrap the bread in tin foil and place in the oven for 10–15 minutes, until the butter has melted.
- Serve immediately.

DINO THE DINOSAUR'S FAVOURITE DISH ....

Spinach – as Popeye will happily tell you – is all about strength. This leaf actually strengthens the brain, eyesight and muscles. Making this an ideal dish for your child's development.

Serves 2–4
Prep time: 10 minutes
Cooking time: 25 minutes

2 tbsp coconut oil
3 chicken breasts, thickly sliced
250g baby spinach
1 red onion
2 tomatoes
2 cloves of garlic
mild curry paste
cumin seeds
4 tbsp cream cheese

- Add a spoon of coconut oil to a frying pan and allow to melt. Then fry the chicken until golden. Remove from the heat and set aside.
- Meanwhile, steam the spinach for a few minutes, until just wilting, then strain. Put the spinach in a food processor and blend until it has a smooth texture. Set to one side.
- Next, blend the onion, tomatoes and garlic with the curry paste (set aside). Add a little oil to a pan and gently heat, throw in the cumin seeds and toast for a minute or so. Wait until they start crackling then pour in the tomato mixture, giving it a good stir. Cover and reduce the heat. Let it simmer for 5–7 minutes, stirring occasionally.
- Once the mixture is cooked, stir in the spinach, cream cheese and chicken and simmer, stirring occasionally, for around 15 minutes.

Mum's Tip: *A great tip for family conversation with this meal is to discuss what dinosaurs ate. You can go through all the different species of dinosaur and try and work out what they liked to eat.*

COCONUT DAHL

This one is ideal for those nights when there isn't much in the fridge. Need to do the weekly shop tomorrow? This is for the night before. It can be kept in the fridge for a few days and reheated if need be, making it a real lifesaver of a dish.

Serves 4-6
Prep time: 10 minutes
Cooking time: 45 minutes

1 tsp coconut oil
1 large red onion, sliced
2 large cloves of garlic, crushed
1 tsp chilli flakes
2 tbsp mild curry powder (or why not spice it up to medium?)
750ml chicken stock
200ml coconut milk
200ml chopped tomatoes
400g red lentils
salt and pepper
2 tbsp chopped coriander, to serve
4-6 naan bread, to serve

• Melt the coconut oil in a frying pan and add the onion. Sauté for around 3-4 minutes until soft. Add the garlic and cook for a further minute. Then add the spices, stock, coconut milk, tomatoes and lentils. Season. Cook for 35-45 minutes until the lentils are soft and sauce thickened. Remove from the heat, sprinkle with coriander and serve with naan bread.

CAULIFLOWER PIZZA

Every kid loves pizza, so swapping the base for cauliflower is a great way to ensure yours are getting something they love to eat as well as enough veg to keep them in tip-top condition.

Serves 4–6
Prep time: 10 minutes
Cooking time: 1 hour

(base)
1 cauliflower
2 eggs
100g ground almonds
sprinkle of cayenne pepper
salt

(toppings)
2 tbsp tomato purée
6 balls of mozzarella
½ red pepper, cut into matchsticks
½ green pepper, cut into matchsticks
½ cup of red onion, thinly sliced
6 large basil leaves, torn
8 slices of pepperoni

- Heat the oven to 200°C/Gas Mark 6. Remove the leaves from the cauliflower and trim the stalk. Cut into chunks.
- Whizz half of the cauliflower in a food processor until it is very fine (like rice). Repeat with the other half.
- Place the cauliflower particles in a non-stick frying pan and cook for 10 minutes, stirring occasionally. When the cauliflower is dry, tip into a large bowl and mix in the eggs, almonds, cayenne pepper and 1 tsp of salt.
- Line a baking tray with greaseproof paper and divide the mixture into two (to make two medium-sized bases or alternately one large). Shape them using a spoon or your fingers. Bake for 30 minutes. The base should have solidified into one golden piece.
- Remove from the oven and, using a palette knife, release the base from the paper. Flip over and cook again for another 10 minutes. When both sides are golden, remove from the oven and spread them with tomato purée. Scatter the torn mozzarella, peppers and red onion over the tomato sauce.
- Sprinkle over the basil and pepperoni. Cook for another 10 minutes.

FRUITY CHICKEN CURRY ....

One of the simplest dishes to make, but with the most awesome, fruity flavour, this excellent curry is full of surprises. And healthy things too! It's really handy for those days when after-school clubs seem to take all night.

Serves 2–4
Prep time: 10 minutes
Cooking time: 25 minutes

2 chicken breasts
1 tbsp rapeseed oil
1 onion, thinly sliced
1 tsp cumin seeds
1 cloves of garlic, crushed
1 tsp ginger, grated
1 tsp tomato purée
1 tsp mild curry powder
1 tsp honey
200ml coconut milk
70g raisins
70g apricots, chopped
½ tsp cornflour

- Cut the chicken into bite-sized pieces. Add the oil to a frying pan and brown the chicken on a gentle heat. Remove and set aside.
- Next, fry the onion and cumin seeds for around 2–3 minutes. Then add the garlic and ginger and cook for a further minute.
- Next add the tomato purée, curry powder, honey and coconut milk and combine well.
- Place the chicken into the mixture and simmer for 10 minutes until the sauce thickens. Then add the raisins and apricots and allow to simmer for a further 5 minutes. If mixture is still a little runny, mix half a tsp of cornflour with a little water and stir in. Allow to thicken and serve.

Mum's Tip: *Make this a really sneaky dish and serve it with cauliflower rice (see page 79)!*

MARVELLOUS MACARONI

There are dozens – if not hundreds – of different recipes for macaroni cheese, but this one is both healthy and tasty and that's not a combination that is easy to come by! The sneaky butternut squash in this recipe is full of dietary fibre, so it's exceptionally heart-friendly. Plus, it's got a ton of potassium and vitamin B6 in it too, which are essential for the proper functioning of the nervous and immune systems.

Serves 4–6
Prep time: 15 minutes
Cooking time: 50 minutes

1 small butternut squash, peeled and diced
2 tbsp rapeseed oil
250g macaroni
60g butter
60g flour
600ml milk
250g Cheddar cheese
50g Parmesan, grated
150g tinned sweetcorn

- Preheat the oven to 200°C/Gas Mark 6 and roast the butternut squash in the rapeseed oil for 30 minutes. Stir occasionally. Once cooked, purée in a food processor and set aside.

- Cook the macaroni in a large pan of boiling water following the pack instructions. While the pasta is cooking, make your white sauce. Over a medium heat melt the butter, stir in the flour and then whisk in the milk. Bring to the boil, stirring constantly before lowering the heat and allowing the mixture to thicken. Remove from the heat and stir in two-thirds of the Cheddar, the Parmesan, sweetcorn and the butternut squash purée. Make sure all the ingredients are combined well.

- Add the macaroni to the sauce and mix and season well. Transfer to a deep suitably sized ovenproof dish and sprinkle the remaining Cheddar cheese over the top. Cook for around 20 minutes and serve straightaway.

HOMEMADE FISH FINGERS WITH MUSHY PEAS ....

Fish fingers are a perennial favourite, but as parents we don't like to let the little ones have them too often. These homemade versions are much healthier than the shop-bought ones, plus they are fun and easy to make so everyone can join in. The ground almonds enhance the goodness of the fish, making them exceedingly healthy.

Serves 2-4
Prep time: 15 minutes
Cooking time: 15 minutes

(fish fingers)
75g plain flour
2 eggs
150g breadcrumbs
100g ground almonds
½ tsp turmeric
**400g skinless, boneless
   haddock, cut into neat,
   thumb-width strips**

(for the peas)
250g fresh garden peas
10g butter
sprinkle of black pepper

- You will need three separate bowls. One should be filled with flour, one with eggs, and the third with the breadcrumbs, almonds and turmeric (combine well). Dip a finger of fish into the flour, then the egg, then the breadcrumb mixture so that they are completely covered. Place on a baking tray lined with greaseproof paper and bake for 15 minutes, turning halfway through.
- While the fish fingers are cooking, you can make your mushy peas. Steam the peas for around 10 minutes, mash with the butter and black pepper and serve with the fish fingers.

Mum's Tip: This is a great way to get the kids involved in the cooking – from making their own fish fingers to mushing up peas, this is one fun recipe!

SNEAKY SPAG BOL

It's quick, it's easy, it's oh-so-sneaky!

Serves 4
Prep time: 10 minutes
Cooking time: 30 minutes

1 tbsp rapeseed oil
1 onion, thinly sliced
2 cloves of garlic, crushed
400g tinned tomatoes
1 tsp oregano
1 carrot, grated
1 small courgette, thinly
  sliced
1 red pepper, thinly sliced
2 handfuls of spinach
500g mince
2 beef stock cubes
20g Parmesan cheese
2 tbsp tomato purée
spaghetti and Parmesan
  cheese, grated, to serve

- Heat the oil in a saucepan and sauté the onion for around 2 minutes. Then add the garlic and sauté for another minute. Pour in the tomatoes, add the oregano, carrot, courgette and pepper and simmer for around 10 minutes. Add the spinach and simmer for another 3 minutes, stirring frequently. Allow to slightly cool before placing in a food processor and puréeing to a smooth sauce.

- Brown the mince, then sprinkle over the stock cubes. Cook for a further minute. Add the sneaky vegetable sauce with 2 tbsp of tomato purée and simmer for around 10 minutes.

- Serve with spaghetti, salad and Parmesan cheese.

HOMEMADE POT NOODLE

Pot Noodle can't be healthy . . . can it? Well, this homemade version definitely can, and it tastes darned good, too!

Serves 1
Prep time: 5 minutes
Cooking time: 10 minutes

70g egg noodles
100ml chicken stock
1 spring onion, finely sliced
1 tbsp grated carrot
1 tbsp sweetcorn
50g shredded cooked
  chicken
1 tbsp Bovril

- Cook the noodles as per the packet instructions, then set aside.
- Make up the stock in a saucepan and add the spring onion, carrot, sweetcorn, chicken and Bovril. Gently simmer for around 3 minutes.
- Add the noodles and allow to thicken. Serve immediately.

NACHOS PACKED WITH VEGGIES

This is one meal guaranteed to put a smile on everyone's face: nachos! These are perfect for sharing when the kids have friends over for dinner.

Serves 4-6
Prep time: 10 minutes
Cooking time: 30 minutes

1 tbsp rapeseed oil
1 red onion, sliced
2 cloves of garlic, crushed
1 red pepper
1 small courgette, finely sliced
1 large carrot, grated
250g mince
2tbsp tomato purée
1 beef stock cube
300g packet corn chips
110g Cheddar cheese, grated
salsa, avocado and soured cream to serve

- Preheat the oven to 200°C/Gas Mark 6.
- Heat the oil in a frying pan, and over a gentle heat cook the onion, garlic and pepper for 2 minutes. Add the courgette and carrot and fry for a further two minutes. When the vegetables are soft, place in a food processor and purée to a smooth consistency, set aside.
- Brown the mince. Add the vegetable mixture, tomato purée and beef stock. Reduce the heat and simmer for around 5-10 minutes (until the stock has thickened).
- Arrange the corn chips on a heatproof plate. Top them with mince and sprinkle the cheese over the top. Bake for 15 minutes.
- Serve with salsa, mashed avocado and sour cream.

CREAMY TUNA PASTA BAKE

This tuna pasta bake is so simple to make and the kids always enjoy helping out with it. Tuna is fantastic as it is full of vitamin B, which helps to build and maintain red blood cells, which in turn promote health and wellbeing. This is a great dish for those lulls between school and their next club!

Serves 4–6
Prep time: 10 minutes
Cooking time: 25 minutes

400g fusilli pasta
1 onion, sliced
40g butter
2 cloves of garlic, crushed
40g plain flour
500ml milk
3 tbsp cream cheese
100ml double cream
fresh chives
100g tinned sweetcorn
400g tinned tuna
200g Cheddar, grated

- Cook the pasta according to the packet instructions. Drain once cooked and set aside.
- Sauté the onion with the butter for around 2 minutes, then add the garlic and sauté for another minute, until softened. On a low heat, add the flour and milk, constantly stirring with a whisk until thickened.
- Remove the pan from the heat and stir in the cream cheese, cream, chives, sweetcorn and half the Cheddar. Season. Stir the cooked pasta and tuna into the sauce. Top with remaining grated cheese and bake for 15 minutes. Serve immediately.

SALMON FISHCAKES

Super-healthy, super-sneaky, super-tasty too! These fishcakes are loaded with broccoli. Broccoli is a great vegetable as it's jam-packed with essential vitamins and minerals, which strengthen children's immune system. Ta-da!

Serves 4
Prep time: 10 minutes
Cooking time: 45 minutes

500g potatoes, cut into chunks
85g broccoli, cut into small florets
2 cooked salmon fillets
1 tbsp mixed herbs
salt and pepper
50g breadcrumbs
2 tbsp rapeseed oil

- Cover the potatoes in boiling water and cook for around 20 minutes, until tender. While the potatoes are cooking, steam the broccoli for around 6 minutes then set aside.
- When the potatoes are cooked, mash in the broccoli and then flake in the salmon. Add the spices and mixed herbs. Season well and shape into 4 cakes. Cover in breadcrumbs.
- Heat the oil in a pan and fry the fishcakes for around 3 minutes on each side until golden. Then bake in the oven for 15 minutes.

Mum's Tip: Serve with Sweet Potato Curly Fries (see page 91) for the ultimate indulgence!

VERY BEST VEGETABLE PIE

Not only does this pie really live up to its name, but it is full of veggies making it a great source of nutrients including fibre, folic acid, potassium and vitamins A, C and E.

Serves 4–6
Prep time: 10 minutes
Cooking time: 45 minutes

1 small butternut squash,
   cut into cubes
1 parsnip, thickly sliced
2 carrots, sliced
40g butter
1 leek, finely sliced
1 green pepper, sliced into
   matchsticks
40g plain flour
400ml milk
80g Cheddar cheese, grated
1 tbsp Parmesan cheese,
   grated
100g peas
salt and pepper
1 sheets of frozen puff
   pastry
1 egg, beaten

- Preheat the oven to 200°C/Gas Mark 6.
- Steam the squash, parsnips and carrots for 10 minutes or until all the veg is tender. Drain and set aside in a bowl.
- Meanwhile, melt the butter in a saucepan over a gentle heat. Add the leek and pepper and cook for 5 minutes, or until soft. Add the flour and stir constantly for about a minute.
- Add the milk, a little at a time, and keep stirring as you do so. Bring to the boil then reduce the heat down to low and simmer for a few minutes to allow the sauce to thicken. Stir in the cheeses. Add the sauce to the bowl of veg along with the peas and mix and season well.
- Transfer everything to a pie dish. Line the pie dish. Make pastry lid. Using a fork, press the two layers together before trimming off the excess pastry. Make a small insertion in the middle of the pie lid to allow the steam to escape, then brush the top with the beaten egg.
- Bake for around 25–30 minutes or until the pie is golden. Serve immediately.

Mum's Tip: Serve with Cauliflower Mash (see page 91) to give your little ones extra nutrients.

RAINBOW SALAD

With this eye-catching salad it will be impossible for the little ones not to notice how good it looks! And there is the added benefit of it being entirely healthy too. In fact, you can talk about the amazing power of vegetables and explain that each colour of vegetable has special powers. For example, red veg is packed full of powerful antioxidants, green vegetables can be high in iron and vitamins A, K and C, and yellow very is good for the immune system.

Serves 2–4
Prep time: 15 minutes
Cooking time: 20 minutes

2 tbsp rapeseed oil
1 tsp oregano
salt and pepper
2 skinless chicken breasts
1 carrot, grated
½ red pepper, finely chopped
½ yellow pepper, finely chopped
2 large handfuls of baby spinach
1 medium avocado
2 spring onions, sliced

- Preheat the grill on a medium heat.
- Take a plastic sandwich bag (or similar) and pour in the oil. Add the oregano and salt and pepper before placing the chicken in the bag, too. Secure the bag at the top and shake well to coat the chicken.
- Grill the chicken until the juices run clear (around 10 minutes on each side).
- While the chicken is cooking, make the salad. Mix the carrot and peppers in a bowl, then add the baby spinach and mix again. You can use your hands for this to make sure all the colours are even.
- Prepare the avocado (remove the stone, remove the flesh and slice and dice into small chunks). Mix the avocado into the salad, then the spring onions.
- Once the chicken is done, remove from the oven and slice into 1cm strips. Divide the salad between the serving plates and place the chicken on top.

Mum's Tip: *Serve with Balsamic Vinegar Dressing (see page 90). Just drizzle over the salad and toss before adding the chicken*

BALSAMIC VINEGAR DRESSING

Prep time: 5 minutes

60ml balsamic vinegar
180ml olive oil
1 tbsp honey

- Place all ingredients into a glass jar, pop on the lid and shake vigorously until thoroughly combined. Use when required.

Sides

CAULIFLOWER MASH

Mashed cauliflower is a great way of sneaking vegetables into your kids' diet, because it is every bit as tasty as regular mash. The bonus is the cauliflower gives them the vitamin C and fibre they need.

Serves 4–6
Prep time: 10 minutes
Cooking time: 20 minutes

1 medium cauliflower, cut into small florets
800g potatoes
60ml double cream
1 tbsp butter
50g grated cheese

- Steam the cauliflower florets for around 10 minutes. Once tender, purée and set aside.
- Meanwhile, cook the potatoes in a pan of boiling water for around 20 minutes or until tender. Drain and return potatoes to the saucepan. Mash in the puréed cauliflower, cream, butter and grated cheese until the mixture reaches your ideal consistency. Serve immediately.

SWEET POTATO CURLY FRIES

Every mum needs a spiralizer! They create noodles, make the veg look pretty, and . . . they make curly fries too.

Serves 2
Prep time: 10 minutes
Cooking time: 25 minutes

2 large sweet potatoes
3 tbsp flour
2 tbsp rapeseed oil

- Preheat the oven to 200°C/Gas Mark 6. Spiralize the potatoes and put them to one side.
- Place the flour in a bowl and dip in the potatoes to cover in flour before placing on a large baking tray, on top of some greaseproof paper. Don't let them touch each other as they will go soggy.
- Drizzle the oil over the fries, making sure they are all covered.
- Place them in the oven and bake for 15 minutes. Carefully take them out and turn, before baking for another 10 minutes. They need to be crispy, but do keep an eye on them because they will easily burn.

SWEET POTATO AND CARROTY MASH

This creamy, buttery mash is so comforting and delicious. My kids adore it! It's packed full of orange veg so you know it's good for them. These bright-coloured root vegetables are packed full of flavonoids, potassium, vitamin C and beta-carotene (vitamin A). The nutrients help our bodies in lots of different ways, from helping us grow to fighting off bugs.

Serves 4–6
Prep time: 10 minutes
Cooking time: 20 minutes

3 large carrots, peeled and chopped
500g sweet potatoes, peeled and chopped
3 tbsp butter
1 tbsp cream
salt and pepper

- Place carrots and potatoes into a steamer and steam for 20 minutes or until tender.
- Remove the veg from the heat and allow to steam-dry for a minute or two. Add the butter and cream and mash. Season and serve immediately.

SKINNY CARROT CHIPS

Apart from the colour, kids aren't always exactly drawn to carrots. But making them into chips will have them asking for more!

Serves 2–4
Prep time: 5 minutes
Cooking time: 45 minutes

500g carrots
2 tbsp flour
1 tbsp rapeseed oil

- Preheat the oven to 200°C/Gas Mark 6. Cut the carrots into thin strips about 1cm thick. Cover the fries in flour and lay them on greaseproof paper on a baking tray.
- Drizzle carrots with oil and season. Bake for 40–45 minutes, turning halfway through. Serve immediately.

CAULIFLOWER AND BROCCOLI CHEESE

This can be a vitamin-filled side dish or a main meal.

Serves 4
Prep time: 10 minutes
Cooking time: 25 minutes

1 tbsp rapeseed oil
4 rashers of streaky bacon
1 small cauliflower, cut into
florets
1 small broccoli, cut into
florets

(sauce)
50g butter
50g flour
400ml milk
1 tsp Dijon mustard
100g Cheddar cheese,
grated
a handful of breadcrumbs

- Preheat the oven to 190°C/Gas Mark 5.
- Fry the streaky bacon in a frying pan for 1-2 minutes on each side. Cut into small pieces and set aside.
- Steam the cauliflower and broccoli for around 5-7 minutes. Drain and transfer to a large ovenproof dish. Mix the bacon into the veg.
- To make the sauce, put the butter, flour and milk in a saucepan on a low heat, whisk continuously. Bring to the boil, then turn the heat down and simmer for a few minutes until the sauce thickens. Add the mustard and cheese and season well.
- Pour the sauce over the vegetables and sprinkle with the breadcrumbs. Cook in the oven for 20 minutes and serve immediately.

Pasta Sauces

Busy mums can never have enough pasta sauces in their arsenal. These dishes are quick and simple to make but still packed full of taste and nutrition.

SPINACH AND RICOTTA PASTA SAUCE

Serves 4
Prep time: 5 minutes
Cooking time: 10 minutes

1 tbsp butter
1 small red onion, finely
  chopped
1 clove of garlic, crushed
250g fresh spinach,
  chopped
200g ricotta cheese
100g grated Cheddar
  cheese
10g grated Parmesan, to
  serve

- Heat the butter in a pan and sauté the onion on a gentle heat for around 3 minutes. Add the garlic and cook for another minute. Add the spinach and cook until the leaves are wilted. Drain.
- Add the ricotta cheese and grated Cheddar and stir, place in a blender and blend until it becomes a lovely smooth sauce. Serve with your favourite pasta and Parmesan cheese.

TOMATO AND MASCARPONE PASTA SAUCE

Serves 2
Prep time: 5 minutes
Cooking time: 25 minutes

1 tbsp rapeseed oil
1 small red onion, finely
  chopped
2 cloves of garlic, crushed
1 tin of chopped tomatoes
2 tsp mixed herbs
1 tbsp tomato purée
100g mascarpone
50g grated cheese
2 tbsp Parmesan
salt and pepper, to season
pasta, to serve

- Place the oil into a frying pan on a gentle heat and sauté the onion for 2 minutes, then add the garlic and fry for a further minute. Add the chopped tomatoes, mixed herbs and tomato purée. Blend in a blender for a few minutes before placing back in the pan. Leave to simmer for around 20-25 minutes, stirring occasionally until the sauce thickens. Stir in the three cheeses until melted.
- Season and serve with your favourite pasta.

SWEET PEPPER PASTA SAUCE

Serves 2
Prep: 5 minutes
Cooking time: 30 minutes

2 tbsp rapeseed oil
½ red onion, finely chopped
1 jar roasted red pepper,
  drained and roughly
  chopped
2 cloves of garlic, crushed
salt and pepper
2 tbsp basil
3 tbsp cream cheese
1 tbsp Parmesan
100ml vegetable stock

- Add the oil to a frying pan and gently sauté the onion for 2 minutes. Add the red peppers and sauté for a further 2 minutes. Then add the garlic and cook for a further minute.
- Remove the pan from the heat and carefully transfer the ingredients (including the basil) to a food processor. Purée the mixture until smooth.
- Pour the purée back in the pan, season well and add the cream cheese, Parmesan and stock. Simmer for 20 minutes to allow to thicken. Serve with your favourite pasta.

SNEAKY VEGETABLE PASTA SAUCE

Serves 2
Prep: 5 minutes
Cooking time: 30 minutes

2 tbsp rapeseed oil
1 celery stick, finely sliced
1 red pepper, deseeded
  and finely chopped
1 yellow pepper, deseeded
  and finely chopped
½ red onion, finely chopped
1 carrot, grated
1 clove of garlic, crushed
1 tin chopped tomatoes
1 tbsp fresh basil, torn
½ tsp mild chilli powder,
  optional

- Sauté the vegetables for around 5-7 minutes, then add the garlic and cook for a further minute. Add the tomatoes, basil and chilli powder (optional) and simmer for around 20 minutes.
- Remove pan from the heat, cool slightly and carefully pour the mixture into a food processor and purée to a smooth consistency. Once you have your desired consistency, warm through and serve with your favourite pasta.

6
DELICIOUS DESSERTS

If your kids regard most vegetables on their plates with suspicion, or even disdain, it might be time to outwit your finicky offspring by sneaking some of those veggies into yummy desserts! Desserts should not be used as substitutes for nutritious, well-balanced meals. However, on days when you decide to treat your family to some scrumptious 'afters', you can also get some nutrient-packed veg like kale, spinach or sweet potatoes into those pernickety little bellies!

BERRY DELIGHT CHEESECAKE

This cheesecake is packed with superstar vitamins and minerals – thanks to the *superfood* berries that are concealed within the luscious, sweet filling!

Serves 8
Prep time: 20 minutes
Chilling time: 1 hour

(for the base)
225g digestive biscuits, crushed
40g sugar
65g butter

(for the filling)
100g strawberries
4 tbsp double cream
500g full-fat cream cheese
1 tsp vanilla essence
100g raspberries
60g icing sugar

- Combine the crushed biscuits and sugar. Melt the butter over a gentle heat and then add it to the bowl. Mix well.
- Spoon the biscuit mixture into a cake tin lined with baking paper. Use a metal spoon to press the mixture down firmly. Chill in the fridge until set.
- Meanwhile, place the strawberries in a blender and blend with the double cream and icing sugar. In a mixing bowl, mix together the cream cheese, vanilla essence and strawberry purée. Then fold in the raspberries.
- Spoon the topping over the chilled biscuit base, making sure it's even and smooth.
- Chill the cheesecake in the fridge for an hour until set.

GREEN SMOOTHIE STRAWBERRY POPS ....

Entice your kids to eat more veg by transforming green smoothies into yummy lollipops. Nutrient-rich spinach blends well into these strawberry smoothie pops.

Makes 6 lollipops
Prep time: 10 minutes
Freezing time: 4–6 hours

200g strawberries, sliced
200ml strawberry yoghurt
100g spinach
200ml vanilla yoghurt
6 lolly moulds

- Blend the strawberries and strawberry yoghurt into a smooth paste and set aside. Clean the blender and then blend the spinach with the vanilla yoghurt. Set aside.
- Using two spoons, first of all spoon the strawberry mixture into each lolly mould to about halfway. Then top up each lolly mould with the spinach mixture using the second spoon.
- Place on the lids and freeze in the freezer for around 4 hours.

Mum's Tip: These lollies are so easy to make. Get your kids to help you make up a batch to freeze – all ready for some tasty refreshment during busy or hot days!

STRAWBERRY COCONUT ICE CREAM

There's something about homemade ice cream that's oh-so-irresistible. I love the intense flavour and creamy texture of this strawberry and coconut ice cream treat: summer in a bowl.

Prep time: 15 minutes
Freezing time: 4 hours

500g strawberries
1 tin (400ml) full-fat coconut milk
500ml double cream
150g coconut sugar (or granulated sugar)
2 tbsp vanilla essence

• Wash the strawberries and then cut each one in half. Place into a blender and blend to a smooth consistency. Set aside.
• Warm the coconut milk over a gentle heat. Add the double cream, vanilla essence and sugar and stir until the sugar has completely dissolved.
• Remove from the heat and then stir in the puréed strawberries. Transfer to the fridge and leave to cool.
• Once the mixture has cooled, place into an ice cream maker and process according to the manufacturer's instructions.

KALE CHOKY POPS

Kids can get their daily dose of essential vitamins along with a yummy chocolate fix with this easy fudge pops recipe!

Makes 8 lollipops
Prep time: 10 minutes
Freezing time: 4–6 hours

1 tin (400ml) coconut milk
50g hot chocolate powder
150g good-quality chocolate
85g double cream
1 tsp vanilla essence
50g kale leaves, stalks removed

• Gently heat the coconut milk and hot chocolate powder in a saucepan until it's blended together. Add the chocolate, broken into pieces, and continue cooking over a gentle heat until the chocolate has melted. Add the double cream and vanilla essence and remove from the heat.
• Place the mixture into a food processor, add the kale and blend until smooth. Divide the mixture between 8 ice pop moulds and insert pop sticks. Freeze for at least 4 hours before serving.

COCONUT AVOCADO TRUFFLES

Great for school lunchboxes. Or enjoy at home – for mid-morning snacks or afternoon tea treats.

Prep time: 1 hour
Chilling time: 30 minutes

1 medium ripe avocado
397g tin condensed milk
1 tsp vanilla extract
100g chopped mixed nuts
220g sweetened shredded coconut
100g dark chocolate

- Peel the avocado, remove the seed and spoon the flesh into a mixing bowl. Using a fork or masher, mash the avocado flesh until it becomes smooth and creamy.
- Stir in the condensed milk, vanilla extract, nuts and most of the shredded coconut. Using your fingers, shape the mixture into small balls. Place the avocado balls onto a baking tray and then pop the tray into the fridge for an hour.
- Once the balls have set, place the chocolate in pieces in a small glass bowl set on top of a saucepan half-filled with boiling water. Melt the chocolate. Dip the balls into the melted chocolate to coat evenly and place onto a fresh baking tray lined with greaseproof paper. Sprinkle with the remaining coconut, pop back in the fridge for 30 minutes and then enjoy!

SWEET POTATO PANCAKES

These nutritious pancakes are ideal for breakfast, lunch, dessert . . .
Your kids will devour them – no persuasion required!

Makes 4 mini pancakes
Prep time: 15 minutes
Cooking time: 40 minutes

100g sweet potato
75ml milk
15g butter
2 beaten eggs
½ tsp vanilla essence
1 banana
75g coconut flour (or plain flour)
1 tbsp rapeseed oil
½ tsp cinnamon

- Peel and dice the sweet potato and then steam for 15–20 minutes until tender. Drain and mash, then set aside.
- Place the milk, butter, eggs, vanilla essence and banana into a food processor and blend to a smooth paste. Add the sweet potato and blend again.
- Sift the flour into a medium bowl. Combine the sweet potato and banana mixtures to form a batter.
- Preheat a little rapeseed oil in a frying pan over a medium heat. Using a big serving spoon, place a quarter of the mixture into the pan. Use the spoon to make a circle with the mixture. Cook for around 3 minutes on each side, turning once with a spatula when the surface begins to bubble.
- Serve immediately with a sprinkle of cinnamon and repeat to make 3 more.

Mum's Tip: *If you need a chocolate hit, add a handful of chocolate chips!*

BANANA YOGHURT BITES

A fresh and fruity dairy treat. Ideal as a filling snack, tangy dessert or a light and refreshing breakfast.

Prep time: 5 minutes
Freezing time: 1 hour

1 large banana
160g vanilla yoghurt
1 tbsp chocolate chips

- Place the banana and yoghurt into a blender and blend until smooth.
- Divide the mixture evenly into 12 cupcake cases on a tray.
- Sprinkle with chocolate chips
- Place the tray into the freezer and leave for an hour or so until the mixture has set solid.

> **Mum's Tip:** These tasty treats can also be used for parties or as light summer snacks.

CAULIFLOWER RICE PUDDING

This grain-free pudding is nutritious, chewy, sweet . . . and surprisingly satisfying.

Serves 4
Prep time: 5 minutes
Cooking time: 10 minutes

1 small head cauliflower
50ml whole milk
50ml double cream
1 tsp vanilla essence
1 tsp ground cinnamon
1 tbsp honey
60g coconut sugar (or granulated sugar)
50g cream cheese
2 eggs, beaten
1 tbsp cornflour, if needed
2 tbsp chocolate chips
flaked almonds, for garnish

- Divide the cauliflower into florets and pulse in a food processor until they look like grains of rice. Gently heat the milk, double cream, vanilla essence, cinnamon, honey and sugar until the sugar has dissolved. Allow to cool and then beat in the cream cheese. Set aside.
- Add the cauliflower to the cream cheese mixture and stir well. Add the beaten egg and gently heat in the pan until the mixture re-thickens. If the mixture is a little runny, mix 1 tbsp of cornflour with a little water and add to the pan. When ready, mix in the chocolate chips.
- Pour into 4 small pots and garnish with flaked almonds. Eat hot, or pop into the fridge for 2 hours and enjoy chilled.

Cakes and Cookies

COURGETTE COOKIES ....

It's great fun to see kids' reactions when they find out these biscuits are packed with grated courgette. It doesn't stop them from eating them – or returning for second helpings!

Makes 16
Prep time: 10 minutes
Cooking time: 15 minutes

200g self-raising flour
250g porridge oats
1 medium courgette, grated
1 tsp cinnamon
170g caster sugar
7g bicarbonate of soda
150g butter
3 tbsp golden syrup

- Preheat the oven to 190°C/Gas Mark 5. Line a baking tray with greaseproof paper.
- Place the flour, oats, grated courgette, cinnamon, sugar and bicarbonate of soda into a medium bowl and mix well. Melt the butter and golden syrup in a pan over a gentle heat. When melted, pour the syrup mixture over the courgette mixture and stir well.
- Roll the mixture into small balls, place onto a baking tray and flatten slightly with a folk or spoon. Bake in the oven for 10 minutes or until golden.
- Allow to cool before serving or storing in an airtight container.

Mum's Tip: *I love playing the guessing game with these cookies. Ask your children to guess as many ingredients in the cookie recipe as they can.*

BLACK BEAN BROWNIES

Guilt-free treats packed with goodness, these black bean brownies contain fibre, protein, iron and magnesium – essential nutrients for little growing bodies.

Prep time: 10 minutes
Cooking time: 20 minutes

175g pitted dates
400g black beans
3 tbsp coconut flour (or plain flour)
1 tbsp peanut butter
3 tbsp hot chocolate
½ tsp baking powder
4 tbsp double cream
2 tbsp chocolate chips

- Soak the dates in a bowl of warm water. Sun-soft dates will need between 5 and 10 minutes. Hard sundried dates will need to be soaked for between 4 and 6 hours. When soft, drain and blend.
- Preheat the oven to 200°C/Gas Mark 6.
- Place all the ingredients apart from the chocolate chips into a food processor. Blend, stopping intermittently if you need to scrape down the sides with a spatula as it's important to make sure everything is combined.
- Once your mixture is smooth, set aside and line a baking tray with greaseproof paper. Place tablespoonfuls of the mixture one at a time onto the tray, sprinkle with a few chocolate chips and flatten with a fork.
- Bake in the oven for 20 minutes. The cookies will be soft when you take them out. Leave them to cool and harden a little before serving.

SPINACH AND CHOCOLATE CHIP MUFFINS

Muffins make delicious snacks, lunchbox treats and puddings. Fruity muffins are delicious, but for a nutritious change, I add some spinach into the mix. Spinach and chocolate chips? It might not sound like a tasty combination, but you can't taste the spinach, which makes it the perfect sneaky veg dessert!

Prep time: 10 minutes
Cooking time: 20 minutes

180g self-raising flour
150g sugar
1 tsp baking powder
70ml rapeseed oil
1 medium egg, beaten
1 tsp vanilla extract
25g spinach
50g chocolate chips

- Heat the oven to 200°C/Gas Mark 6. Line a muffin tray with paper cake liners.
- Mix the flour, sugar and baking powder in a bowl. In a separate bowl, whisk together the oil, egg and vanilla extract. Add the liquid mixture to the dry ingredients and combine. Blend in the spinach with a hand-held whisk until the mixture reaches a smooth consistency. Add the chocolate chips and mix well.
- Spoon the mixture into the cake cases. Bake the muffins for 15 to 20 minutes, or until a toothpick inserted into the middle of a muffin comes out with crumbs, not wet batter. Transfer the muffins to a cooling rack and allow to cool before serving.

7

GLUTEN-FREE

Only a few years ago, the word 'gluten' would have meant little, if anything, to most people. Today, discussions about gluten and its related topics such as gluten intolerance and gluten-free foods have become part of everyday conversations. Chatter about gluten takes place not only on celebrity Twitter feeds and within newspapers and magazines but, increasingly, among parents in places like school playgrounds and via online settings such as parenting forums and 'mummy blogs'.

WHAT IS GLUTEN?

Gluten is the name given to a family of proteins that are found in grains like wheat, rye, barley and spelt. The two main proteins in gluten are called glutenin and gliadin and, of these, gliadin causes the most health problems for those who are sensitive to gluten or have coeliac disease.

Gluten proteins in flour become sticky when the flour is mixed with water and this glue-like stickiness makes the dough stretchy and causes it to rise when baked. Gluten can be found in many different food products, and the following list represents only a small selection: pasta, noodles, cereals, crackers, cookies, soups, pastries, sauces, couscous and sweets. If you are gluten-intolerant, your sensitivity can also be triggered by foods that do not contain gluten but which have been exposed to gluten via cross-contact, for example via shared utensils. Cross-contact contamination might occur in places like bakeries where airborne wheat flour particles can settle onto surfaces, utensils and uncovered food products.

GLUTEN INTOLERANCE

The full spectrum of gluten sensitivity ranges from mild reactions such as fatigue to the more serious symptoms brought on by coeliac disease – the most severe form of gluten intolerance. According to research carried out by the University of Nottingham, there has been a 'fourfold increase in the rate of diagnosed cases of coeliac disease in the United Kingdom over the past two decades'. Symptoms of coeliac disease include bloating, diarrhoea, nausea, tiredness, muscle wasting, abdominal distension, constipation and headaches. If undiagnosed, symptoms can worsen, and this can be especially concerning when it affects fast-growing children who need optimum nutrition, because the disease can lead to poor appetite and a consequent failure to grow and thrive.

If your child has coeliac disease and eats food that contains gluten, the immune system reacts to the gluten leading to damage of the gut lining. Before diagnosis, children often begin to feel very unwell. Unpleasant symptoms such as bloating and nausea may worsen after eating and children might then begin to form a link in their minds between food and feeling poorly, causing them to lose their appetite and even avoid eating. Symptoms occur only if gluten is eaten; by avoiding gluten, the gut will heal and the child can begin to feel well again.

If your child is gluten-intolerant, he or she can still eat many foods that are naturally gluten-free, including:

- meat
- fish
- fruit and vegetables
- rice
- potatoes
- lentils

Oats can present problems for those with gluten sensitivity. Oats contain a protein called avenin, which is similar to gluten. Most people with coeliac disease can eat avenin without experiencing health problems, according to Coeliac.org.uk. However, problems can occur from eating oats that have been produced alongside gluten-containing grains like wheat, barley and rye and which have consequently become contaminated. Because people with coeliac disease can only eat uncontaminated oats, it makes sense to buy oats and oat products that are certified as gluten-free. Furthermore, a small number of people with coeliac disease are unlucky enough to be sensitive even to oat products that are completely gluten-free!

You can also choose from an array of packaged foods that are labelled 'gluten-free' among supermarket shelves; however, like many processed and packaged foods, these products may have additives and preservatives and, most likely, don't taste as good as home-cooked food.

Many mums are eager to try recipes that avoid wheat or gluten. Following a gluten-free diet doesn't mean you can't be creative in the kitchen. There are plenty of dishes that are safe to eat and many more that can be made gluten-free by following a few simple steps.

The gluten-free recipes in this chapter are easy to prepare. Plus the results look wonderful, taste scrumptious and are packed with nutrients to help you and your family stay healthy.

Get ready to have some gluten-free fun in the kitchen!

Breakfasts

Breakfast is the most important meal of the day, so it's best to fuel up your little ones first thing in the morning with a super-tasty, power-packed meal.

BANANA PANCAKES

These pancakes are super-delicious and quick to make for a healthy breakfast or delicious snack at any time of day.

Serves 2 (makes 2 large pancakes or 4 minis)
Prep time: 2 minutes
Cooking time: 6 minutes

1 large ripe banana
2 large eggs
1 tsp cinnamon
2 tsp coconut oil

- Blend the banana, eggs and cinnamon in a food processor to a smooth consistency.
- Gently heat one teaspoon of the oil in a non-stick frying pan. When the oil has melted, pour half the mixture into the pan.
- Cook on one side for around 3 minutes (or until the bottom looks golden-brown when you lift up one of the corners). Flip the pancake gently onto the other side and cook for a further few minutes. Serve immediately.
- Follow the same method with any leftover mixture.

Mum's Tip: I love sprinkling ground almonds onto one side of the pancake when cooking. It gives a lovely nutty flavour.

SWEET MINI OMELETTES

Traditional-style breakfast choices consist of toast and cereals, which tend to be full of wheat and oats. It can take a while to adjust to eating breakfasts that are without bread or cereal. Eggs in all forms, such as omelettes, are an excellent alternative.

Makes 12
Prep time: 10 minutes
Cooking time: 30 minutes

2 large eggs
1 small banana
1 apple, grated
1 tsp sugar
½ tsp cinnamon
½ tbsp rapeseed oil (for greasing)

- Preheat the oven to 190°C/Gas Mark 5.
- Place the eggs and banana into a blender and blend for a minute or so before pouring into a bowl. Add the apple. Mix in the sugar and cinnamon.
- Grease a muffin tin with vegetable oil and pour the mixture into each muffin cup, until the cup is almost, but not quite, full. Place in the oven and bake for 30 minutes, or until the omelettes are golden on top.

Mum's Tip: I cook up a big batch of these as they are great for lunchboxes too. I often use silicone cake cases as sometimes the omelettes can get stuck in the muffin tin even if they have been well greased.

HOT QUINOA CEREAL WITH BLUEBERRIES AND MAPLE SYRUP ....

Quinoa makes a healthy, gluten-free breakfast. Just right for getting kids energised for their day ahead.

Serves 2
Prep time: 5 minutes
Cooking time: 10 minutes

220ml coconut milk
35g quinoa flakes
1 tbsp honey
2 tbsp double cream
½ tsp ground cinnamon
100g blueberries

• Bring the coconut milk to a boil in a large saucepan over a high heat. Stir in the quinoa flakes and cook them according to the instructions on the pack. When cooked, remove from the heat and stir in the honey and double cream. Sprinkle over the cinnamon. Leave to stand for 3–5 minutes or until slightly thickened.
• When ready, stir in the blueberries and serve.

BERRY CRUNCH ....

Everything about this delicious breakfast is good. It even looks beautiful! Seeds and berries are full of nutrients and provide a healthy dose of antioxidants, too. Adding a dollop of natural yoghurt makes this the breakfast of champions!

Serves 2-4
Prep time: 5 minutes
Cooking time: 5 minutes

35g pumpkin seeds
35g sunflower seeds
35g ground linseeds
35g chopped walnuts
1 tsp vanilla extract
60g blueberries
60g strawberries
60g raspberries
4 tbsp plain yoghurt,
to serve

• Preheat the oven to 180°C/Gas Mark 4. Place the seeds and nuts on a baking tray and bake for around 5 minutes, turning occasionally to stop them from burning.
• Pour them into a large bowl and add the vanilla extract and berries. Stir well, then serve with the plain yoghurt on the top.

GLUTEN-FREE GRANOLA

The ingredients in granola make it the ultimate anxiety-buster – great for getting kids off to a good start on days when they have school tests or exams! The ingredients in this recipe are renowned for supporting the nervous system during stressful situations. Foods such as gluten-free oats have an effect on neurotransmitters in the brain (including the hormone serotonin, which is why they leave you feeling so good once you've eaten them). Breakfast is important, and providing a breakfast like this is one of the best ways you can help your child prepare for a healthy, positive day.

Serves 4–6
Prep time: 5 minutes
Cooking time: 30 minutes

170g certified gluten-free rolled oats
55g almonds, chopped
55g walnuts, chopped
55g sunflower seeds
55g pumpkin seeds
55g flax seeds
55g coconut, shredded
2 tbsp coconut oil
3 tbsp honey
1 tsp ground cinnamon
2 tsp vanilla extract
55g dried cranberries
55g dried raisins

- Preheat the oven to 180°C/Gas Mark 4. Combine the gluten-free oats, nuts, seeds and coconut together in a large bowl.
- In a saucepan, combine the coconut, coconut oil, honey, cinnamon and vanilla. Heat the mixture gently until the honey is just soft and everything is mixed. Remove from the heat, pour over the oaty mixture and combine well.
- Line a baking tray with baking paper and spread the granola over it. Bake for 20–25 minutes, checking every 10 minutes and moving it around on the tray if necessary (to ensure it all browns evenly). When the granola is golden-brown, take out of the oven and let it cool. Add the raisins and cranberries. Serve with almond milk and store the leftovers in an airtight container for future use.

Snacks

FRUIT AND CHEESE KABOBS ....

I love making fruit kabobs with my kids. I love the taste of pineapple and cheese – it reminds me of yesteryear children's parties! These are easy to make and kids love to help prepare them. I ask my children to cut the cheese into small stars or heart shapes.

Makes 6
Prep time: 10 minutes

2 kiwi fruits
¼ pineapple
12 grapes, deseeded and halved
12 thick slices of cheese
6 skewers

• Peel and cut the kiwi into 2cm chunks. Peel and cut the pineapple into 2cm chunks. (Any leftovers can be placed in a bowl on the table or stored in the fridge for up to 3 days.) Get your children to use a small star cookie cutter to cut the cheese into star shapes. Thread the fruits onto a skewer and serve immediately.

PEANUT BUTTER AND BANANA RICE CAKES ....

Your kids will go nuts for this nutritious snack. The combination of peanut butter and fruit is yummy, plus it's quick and easy to make.

Makes 2
Prep time: 10 minutes

6 strawberries
1 small banana
2 tbsp of my Homemade Peanut Butter (see page 14)
2 large rice cakes

• Remove the stalks from the strawberries and slice them into quarters. Slice the banana and set aside. Spread the peanut butter over the rice cakes and then place the strawberries and banana slices on top. Serve straightaway.

GLUTEN-FREE ENERGY BARS

Everyone loves a tasty energy bar! This gluten-free version is particularly irresistible and, because of the nuts, highly nutritious.

Makes 12
Prep time: 10 minutes
Cooking time: 30 minutes

200g gluten-free oats
100g sunflower seeds
50g pine nuts
50g chopped walnuts
150g butter
5 tbsp honey
1 tsp cinnamon
85g coconut sugar (or granulated sugar)
50g dried cranberries
50g dried apricots, cut into small chunks
50g shredded coconut

- Preheat the oven to 180°C/Gas Mark 4.
- Mix together the oats, seeds and nuts in a bowl and bake in the oven for around 5–10 minutes (but no longer than this because they burn quickly).
- While the dry ingredients are cooking, heat the butter, honey, cinnamon and sugar gently in a pan, stirring all the time until melted.
- When the dry ingredients are lightly toasted, remove them from the oven and place into a bowl. Remove the wet ingredients from the heat and add them to the dry mixture. Stir well, add the fruit and stir well again.
- Grease and line a medium baking tray. Transfer the mixture to the tray by spreading it evenly and pressing down firmly with the back of a spoon. Alternatively, place a piece of baking paper over the mixture and use another tray to press down really firmly so the mixture is packed in tight. Then remove the tray and paper.
- Bake in the oven for 20 minutes or until golden-brown. Cool completely before slicing into bars.

BAKED CINNAMON APPLE CRISPS

These scrumptious, fruity chips will disappear almost as quickly as you make them! They're perfect for healthy snacks and also very easy to prepare.

Serves 4
Prep time: 10 minutes
Cooking time: 45 minutes

2 Pink Lady apples, cored and sliced finely
1 tsp ground cinnamon
1 tsp coconut sugar (or granulated sugar)

• Preheat oven to 200°C/Gas Mark 6. Place the apple slices onto a lined baking tray. Mix the cinnamon and coconut sugar in a bowl and then sprinkle it over the apples. Cook for around 45 minutes or until golden. You can tell these are ready when they look dried out and the ends start to curl. Remove from the oven and allow them to cool and go crispy.

Lunches

COCONUT WAFFLE ....

Just because your child cannot eat wheat, doesn't mean you have to give up flour as there are lots of alternatives. This recipe is made with coconut flour, which is packed with protein and fibre, making it a nutritious alternative to wheat flour.

Serves 2
Prep time: 15 minutes
Cooking time: 5 minutes

70g coconut flour (or plain flour)
1 tbsp baking powder
1 tsp cinnamon
170ml coconut milk
5 tbsp butter
1 small banana
2 large eggs
2 tbsp honey
1 tsp vanilla extract

- Mix together all the dry ingredients. Place the rest of the ingredients in a food processor and blend.
- Pour the wet mixture onto the dry ingredients and mix well. Let the mixture rest for 5–10 minutes. While the mixture is resting, turn on your waffle iron and allow it to preheat.
- Once the waffle iron is heated, pour the batter onto the waffle tray, making sure the surface is covered. Cook for 3–4 minutes or until golden.
- Repeat with the remaining mixture and serve with maple syrup or honey.

Mum's Tip: *I love adding a dollop of Greek yoghurt and blueberries.*

COURGETTE FRITTERS

These veggie gluten-free fritters are packed with flavour. Serve them on their own or as a side dish with sausages.

Makes 4
Prep time: 10 minutes
Cooking time: 10 minutes

2 tbsp rapeseed oil
1 red onion, finely sliced
2 cloves of garlic, crushed
1 courgette, grated
50g flour
100g grated Parmesan cheese
2 eggs
1 tsp mixed herbs and spices

- Gently heat 1 tbsp of the oil and fry the onion for a few minutes before adding the garlic and sautéing for a further minute.
- In a bowl, combine the grated courgette, flour and Parmesan with the cooked onion and garlic, mix well before beating in the eggs and herbs. Shape into small balls and flatten.
- Pour the rest of the oil into a non-stick frying pan and fry the fritters for 2–3 minutes on each side or until golden.

TOMATO EGGS

Making scrambled eggs with your kids is fun, scrumptious and will always go down a treat. Sneaking tomatoes in will also vamp up the nutritional content – enjoy!

Serves 2
Prep time: 5 minutes
Cooking time: 5–10 minutes

2 tsp butter
1 clove garlic, crushed
200g chopped tomatoes
small handful fresh basil
1 tbsp grated Parmesan cheese, plus extra to serve
4 eggs, beaten

- Melt the butter in a non-stick pan, add the garlic and tomatoes and then simmer for a few moments. Stir in the Parmesan and basil.
- Add the eggs to the pan. Stir the mixture as it cooks until the eggs are scrambled.
- Serve with a sprinkle of Parmesan.

STUFFED SWEET POTATO

This recipe is a family favourite – we have this meal at least once a week. Sweet potatoes are so tasty and extremely nutritious for kids.

Serves 2
Prep time: 10 minutes
Cooking time: 45 minutes

2 medium sweet potatoes
1 tbsp rapeseed oil
2 slices of smoked bacon, diced
1 small red onion, finely chopped
1 clove garlic, crushed
60g feta cheese, cut into small cubes
1 tsp dried oregano
10g Cheddar cheese, grated
handful of chopped parsley

- Preheat the oven to 200°C/Gas Mark 6. Pierce each sweet potato several times with a fork. Place the potatoes directly in the middle of the oven on a baking tray lined with tin foil.
- Bake the potatoes for about 40–50 minutes (depending on their size). When ready, the potatoes will be tender and easy to pierce with a knife. Allow the potatoes to cool a little until you can handle them easily.
- While the potatoes are baking, make the stuffing. Gently fry the bacon in the pan for a few minutes on each side until golden. Remove, then set aside.
- Fry the onion for a few minutes before adding the garlic and frying for a further minute. When cooked, transfer to a bowl and add the bacon. Add the feta cheese and oregano and mix well.
- When the potatoes are cooked, slice lengthways and remove the soft potato insides. Mix the potato insides into the stuffing mixture. Place the potato and stuffing mixture back into the potato skins, sprinkle with cheese and grill for a few minutes.
- Garnish with parsley. Serve straightaway.

Dinners

CORIANDER AND COCONUT SALMON ....

The fish is gently poached in a spicy coconut broth. Your family will love this tender and tasty fish dish.

Serves 2
Prep time: 5 minutes
Cooking time: 20 minutes

1 tbsp rapeseed oil
2 cloves of garlic, crushed
200ml coconut cream
1 tsp mild curry powder
3 spring onions, finely sliced
cornflour, optional
2 salmon fillets
1 tbsp coriander, to garnish

- Place the oil in a pan and gently sauté the garlic for a minute. Place the coconut cream, curry powder and spring onions into a saucepan and gently simmer for a few minutes. Add a little cornflour, mixed into a little cream (or water), to thicken the sauce.
- Place the fish into a baking dish and pour over the warm coconut sauce. Cover with foil and bake for 12–15 minutes.
- Sprinkle with coriander and serve.

Mum's Tip: This tastes great with cauliflower rice (see page 79).

HERBY STUFFED CHICKEN

Chicken has always been a favourite in my household. My kids love this stuffed chicken recipe that's packed full of flavour.

Prep time: 10 minutes
Cooking time: 30 minutes

2 tbsp cream cheese
30g green olives, each
  sliced into 4
3 sundried tomatoes, cut
  into small strips
2 cloves crushed garlic
1 tsp basil
2 chicken breasts
4 slices Parma ham
2 tbsp rapeseed oil

- Preheat the oven to 190°C/Gas Mark 5. Mix the cream cheese, green olives, sundried tomatoes, garlic and basil in a bowl. Flatten the chicken breasts and open each one with a small slit.
- Place a heaped spoonful of the mixture into each chicken breast. Fold the chicken breast back up and press tightly.
- Wrap the Parma ham around the chicken breasts. Place the wrapped chicken breasts onto a greased baking tray and drizzle with oil. Cook in the centre of the oven for 30 minutes or until tender and completely cooked through.

Mum's Tip: Serve with vegetables as a side dish to help familiarise your little ones with different kinds of vegetables.

LEMON AND HERB CHOPS

Lamb chops are quick and easy to cook. The meat is tender and juicy and best served slightly pink. Adding a dash of lemon and herbs to the mix makes this dish oh-so-lovely!

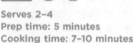

Serves 2–4
Prep time: 5 minutes
Cooking time: 7–10 minutes

1 tbsp rapeseed oil
4 small lamb chops
2 garlic cloves, crushed
2 tsp mixed herbs
juice of ½ lemon

- Gently heat the oil in a pan, cook the lamb on one side for 3 minutes and then on the other side for two minutes. Add the garlic and sauté for a few moments longer. Sprinkle the mixed herbs on top of the chops. Transfer to plates and then squeeze the lemon juice over the meat. Serve immediately.

Mum's Tip: *This recipe tastes delicious with minty new potatoes.*

VEGGIE QUINOA

Labelled as a superfood, quinoa is a complete protein, which makes it ideal for growing bodies. Kids love this gluten-free vegetarian dinner: it's full of different vegetables, which makes it look very colourful and appetising.

Serves 4
Prep time: 5 minutes
Cooking time: 25 minutes

1 tsp rapeseed oil
1 small red onion, finely sliced
1 small head of broccoli, cut into florets
½ butternut squash, diced into small pieces
1 large carrot, grated
2 cloves garlic, crushed
120g quinoa
600 ml vegetable stock
1 tbsp double cream
70g Cheddar cheese
salt and pepper

- Pour the oil into a frying pan and gently sauté the onion, broccoli, squash and carrot for 2-3 minutes before adding the garlic and cooking for an extra minute.
- Add the quinoa and vegetable stock, increase the heat and bring to the boil. Cover the pot and reduce the heat so that the mixture simmers gently.
- Cook for 15-25 minutes until the quinoa is tender and all the stock has been absorbed. Stir in the cream and cheese. Season well and serve.

Desserts

SNEAKY CHOCOLATE MOUSSE

This rich, glossy chocolate mousse is simply delicious!

Serves 4
Prep time: 5 minutes

1 small ripe avocado
1 heaped tbsp Nutella
1 heaped tbsp peanut butter
2 tbsp water
2 tbsp double cream

• Place all the ingredients into a food processor and blend them into a smooth mixture. Keep the mousse chilled and serve it when desired.

Mum's Tip: Place strawberries on top for an even tastier pudding.

BAKED BANANAS

Bananas, the nation's favourite raw snack, are endlessly versatile in the kitchen. This recipe is a little naughty and will surely satisfy any sweet tooth.

Prep time: 5 minutes
Cooking time: 10 minutes

2 medium ripe bananas, skins on
70g dark chocolate, roughly broken
20g raisins
40g chopped walnuts

• Preheat the oven to 180°C/Gas Mark 4. Slice down the inside curve of each banana skin, taking care to avoid cutting right through. Open the bananas out a little. Set aside.
• Fill the bananas with the chocolate, raisins and nuts
• Place the bananas onto a baking sheet and cook in the centre of the oven for 10 minutes or until they are heated through.
• Remove banana skins and serve.

COCONUT RICE PUDDING

This is a simple, creamy rice pudding that tastes amazing.

Serves 4
Prep time: 5 minutes
Cooking time: 40 minutes

75g pudding rice (Pudding rice can be found in the rice section in most supermarkets.)
1 400ml tin coconut milk
300ml full-fat milk
4 tbsp coconut sugar (or granulated sugar)
1 tsp vanilla extract
1 tsp cinnamon
1 large banana, sliced
200g blueberries, halved

- Place the rice, coconut milk, milk, coconut sugar, vanilla extract and cinnamon into a medium pan. Stir well. Cover the pan and simmer the mixture over a gentle heat for around 40 minutes, stirring often, until the rice is tender and starts to thicken.
- Once cooked, spoon the rice into bowls and place the fruit on top.

8
PARTY FOOD

Aren't parties fantastic? They are a time of laughter, fun and of family and friends . . . Food is a huge part of these celebrations, which is an exciting prospect in itself, especially when it comes to children's parties. The food needs to be interesting, cleverly thought out and tasty but, apart from this, it can also be healthy (although a little sugar here and there is fine – it's a party, after all).

In the past, children's parties have been synonymous with fatty, sugary food that isn't great for our health. But there are ways to end this problem, and it's not as difficult as you first may think. The food doesn't have to be limited, nor does it need to be tasteless, but it can still be good for us just the same.

Kids don't want their party food to be healthy – that's the truth of it. But, as always with children's food, what they don't know won't hurt them; in fact, it could even make them healthier!

Here are some great ideas that will help you avoid the junk with minimum fuss!

Savoury Sensations

MINI CHEESY RICE CAKES ....

These little rice cakes may be simple, but they are always a big hit. Fun and healthy in equal measures, they make a change from the traditional sandwich.

Makes 8-10
Prep time: 10 minutes
Cooking time: 15–20 minutes

250g long-grain rice
2 tbsp rapeseed oil
1 small onion, finely sliced
1 clove of garlic, crushed
50g halloumi, diced
25g Parmesan
100g sweetcorn
1 egg
5 tbsp coconut flour (or
   plain flour)
salt and pepper

- Cook the rice according to the packet instructions and put to one side to cool.
- Pour the oil in a pan and heat gently. Add the onion and sauté for 3 minutes before adding the garlic and cooking for another minute. Remove from the pan and set aside.
- Add the diced halloumi, Parmesan, sweetcorn, egg and flour to the onion and garlic, season and mix well. Don't worry if the mixture is wet – it is meant to be.
- Place a little more oil in the pan and dollop in a tablespoon of the mixture. Flatten a little and repeat until the frying pan is full. It may need multiple batches. Cook for 3 minutes on each side. Once cooked remove from the pan and place on a piece of kitchen towel.
- Serve warm.

SWEET CHICKEN NUGGETS

Who doesn't love a chicken nugget or five? These homemade nuggets are super-scrumptious. The fab thing about chicken is that it's great for children due to its rich source of protein and calcium, which keeps their bones strong.

Serves 4
Prep time: 10 minutes
Cooking time: 20 minutes

2 chicken breasts
3 tbsp plain flour
2 eggs, beaten
300g breadcrumbs
100g tinned sweetcorn
1 tbsp rapeseed oil

- Preheat the oven to 190°C/Gas Mark 5.
- Poach the chicken in lightly boiling water for around 5–7 minutes. Don't overcook it as it can easily become dry.
- In the meantime, get three bowls and fill one with the flour, one with the eggs, and the final one with the breadcrumbs.
- When the chicken is cooked, slice when cool enough to handle and place into a food processor. Blend for a minute or two, then add the sweetcorn and pulse until it is smooth. When done, shape spoonfuls of the mixture into nugget shapes. Dip each nugget into the flour, then the egg, then the breadcrumbs.
- Brush a little oil over each nugget and bake for 15 minutes, turning halfway through.

MINI SWEET POTATO BURGERS

Imagine trying to cater for a party that Is just a bunch of fussy eaters. That's pretty much what a kids' party is like. Adults tend to eat what they're given (unless they have allergies), even if they aren't too keen . . . Children, on the other hand, are brutally honest! These little burgers should satisfy everyone though!

Makes 12–14
Prep time: 1 hour
Cooking time: 30 minutes

(buns)
200g bread flour
7g sachet dried yeast
1 tsp salt
1 tsp sugar
5g butter
100ml water
1 egg, beaten
sesame seeds

(burgers)
3 tbsp rapeseed oil
1 small onion, finely chopped
100g sweet potato, grated
1 glove of garlic, crushed
250g minced beef
1 tsp Worcestershire sauce
1 tsp tomato purée
1 egg
50g breadcrumbs
20g ground almonds
slices of Cheddar cheese, to serve

- Preheat the oven to 200ºC/Gas Mark 6.
- Place the flour, yeast, salt, sugar and butter in a bowl. Rub in the butter. Add enough water to form a dough (don't worry if you don't use all the water mentioned in the list of ingredients).
- Place the dough onto a lightly floured surface and knead until smooth and elastic. This takes around 10 minutes.
- Transfer the dough to a lightly oiled bowl, cover with cling film, and set aside in a warm place for about 30 minutes (allowing the dough to double in size).
- Divide the dough into 12–14 small balls and flatten slightly. Place them on greaseproof paper on a baking tray, making sure to leave plenty of space on each side. These may need to be done in batches. Brush each bun with a little beaten egg and sprinkle the top with sesame seeds. Bake for 15 minutes or until golden. Once the rolls are cooked, set aside.
- Meanwhile, make the burgers. Heat the oil in a frying pan and fry the onion and sweet potato for around 3 minutes. Add the garlic and fry for a further minute. Remove from the heat and set aside.
- Mix the mince, Worcestershire sauce and tomato purée in a bowl before adding the onion and sweet potato mixture. Add the egg and mix well.

- Finally, place the breadcrumbs on a plate. Take a small ball of the mince mixture and cover with breadcrumbs and almonds. Roll and flatten and set aside.
- Make up 12-14 mini burgers. Fry with a little oil for 3-4 minutes on each side. Serve with a mini roll and cheese. Place a cocktail stick through the middle to keep in place!

MINI SPRING ROLLS

So moreish, so delicious, the kids (and adults) will go crazy for these surprisingly healthy little bites.

Makes 12
Prep time: 10 minutes
Cooking time: 20 minutes

1 tbsp rapeseed oil
3 spring onions, thinly sliced lengthways
1 large carrot, grated
1 red pepper, cut into matchsticks
2 cloves of garlic, crushed
3 tbsp light soy sauce
100g beansprouts
1 tbsp red wine vinegar
2 sheets of filo pastry, each sheet cut into 6 rectangles
1 egg, beaten

- Preheat the oven to 200°C/Gas Mark 6.
- Place the oil into a frying pan and heat gently. Sauté the onion, carrot and pepper for around 3 minutes. Add the garlic, soy sauce, beansprouts and red wine vinegar and cook for a further 2 minutes.
- Place a spoonful of cooked veg at the bottom of each rectangle of filo pastry. Roll the pastry up, pinching each end to make a seal. Brush with egg and put on a baking try lined with greaseproof paper.
- Bake for 15-20 minutes until golden.

Mum's Tip: *I recommend dipping these in my Sweet Chilli Sauce (see page 48).*

LOVELY LITTLE OMELETTES ....

Ooh, omelettes! There is something about a tasty savoury omelette that kids love, and they can be served either hot or cold, so they are the perfect party snack.

Makes 12
Prep time: 5 minutes
Cooking time: 25 minutes

100g cherry tomatoes, quartered
yellow pepper cut into matchsticks
1 tbsp rapeseed oil
4 eggs
100g sweetcorn
70g Cheddar cheese
salt and pepper

- Preheat the oven to 190°C/Gas Mark 5.
- Place the cherry tomatoes and pepper into a roasting tin and roast with a little oil for 10 minutes. In a jug, whisk up the eggs and then add the roasted veg, sweetcorn and Cheddar cheese. Season well.
- Grease a muffin tray before pouring in the mixture, leaving around 1cm free at the top of each mould as the mixture will rise. Bake for around 15 minutes.
- Serve immediately.

TINY PITTA PIZZAS ....

These tiny pitta pizzas are fantastic to serve at parties or special celebrations. They are just the right size for kids' little tummies ... but beware! They are so delicious everyone is likely to want seconds!

Makes 8
Prep time: 5 minutes
Cooking time: 10 minutes

2 pitta breads, halved and cut into half, to make 8
3 tbsp tomato purée
1 small red onion, finely diced
100g sweetcorn
4 slices of ham, shredded
100g pineapple, sliced into tiny chunks
50g Cheddar cheese, grated

- Preheat oven to 200°C/Gas Mark 6.
- Warm the pittas in the oven for around 1 minute, or until soft. Take out of the oven and spread the tomato purée over each pitta. Sprinkle the onion, sweetcorn, ham, pineapple and, finally, the cheese over the top. Season well.
- Spread the pittas on a large baking tray and cook for around 8 minutes. Serve immediately or wait until cooled.

ROASTED CHICKPEAS

We all know chickpeas make the most intensely flavoursome hummus, but did you also know that when they are roasted they become crisp and transform into a highly nutritious snack?

Prep time: 5 minutes
Cooking time: 30 minutes

400g tinned chickpeas
2 tbsp rapeseed oil
2 tsp smoked paprika

- Preheat the oven to 200°C/Gas Mark 6.
- Drain the chickpeas and pat dry with a clean tea towel. Mix the oil and smoked paprika in a bowl and coat the chickpeas. Place them on a baking tray and season.
- Place the tray in the centre of the oven and roast for around 25-30 minutes, until the chickpeas are golden. Shake the tray every 10 minutes or so. Some of the chickpeas may actually pop, but don't worry – this is totally normal.

CHICKEN ROLLS

What's healthier than a sausage roll? Well, depending on the sausage roll itself, lots of things! One of those things is a chicken roll, a chicken version of its sausage cousin.

Makes 12–14
Prep time: 10 minutes
Cooking time: 45 minutes

1 tbsp rapeseed oil
1 small red onion
½ red pepper, cut into
  matchsticks
1 carrot, grated
2 cloves of garlic, crushed
250g minced chicken
40g grated Parmesan
2 sheets of puff pastry
1 egg, beaten
2 tbsp sesame seeds

- Preheat oven to 200°C/Gas Mark 6.
- Gently heat the oil in a frying pan and sauté the onion, pepper and carrots for around 3 minutes. Add the garlic and cook for another minute. Remove with a slotted spoon and set aside. Then cook the chicken mince. When the chicken mince is cooked, add the onion, pepper and carrot mix, making sure the sautéed vegetables are mixed in well.
- In a bowl, place the chicken mix and Parmesan and give it a good stir. Cut the puff pastry sheets lengthways into two even rectangles. Place the chicken mixture evenly down the centre of each rectangle. Fold one side of the pastry over, making sure the filling is covered. Press down with your fingers to seal and cut away any leftover pastry.
- Once you have a long sausage, cut into 3cm rolls. Bush the individual rolls with some beaten egg and sprinkle the top with sesame seeds.
- Bake for around 30 minutes, or until golden.

TANGY CHEESE STRAWS

Is it even possible to have a party without the quintessential cheese straw? They are delicious for eating just as they are or dipping in our sneaky dips.

Prep time: 10 minutes
Cooking time: 15 minutes

50g cream cheese
35g grated Parmesan
2 tbsp tomato purée
1 sheet of puff pastry
1 egg, beaten

- Preheat the oven to 200°C/Gas Mark 6.
- Mix the cream cheese, Parmesan and tomato purée. Roll out the pastry on a lightly floured surface and cut in half lengthways. Spread the cream cheese mix over one half and then cover with the other half to create a sandwich.
- Cut in half and divide into 1cm-thick strips. Twist each pastry strip and place on a baking tray on top of greaseproof paper. Brush each one with egg, then bake for around 20 minutes or until golden.

PUMPKIN BREADSTICKS

A definitely must at any party and perfect for little ones of all ages.

Makes 10–12
Prep time: 45 minutes
Cooking time: 15–20 minutes

75g butter
280g pumpkin seed bread mix
7g sachet yeast
1 tbsp baking powder
1 tsp salt
220ml milk

- Preheat oven to 220°C/Gas Mark 7.
- Melt the butter. Set aside. Line a baking tray with greaseproof paper.
- In a bowl, mix the bread mix, yeast, baking powder and salt. Stir in the milk and mix well. On a floured surface, knead the mixture lightly for around 10 minutes. Once kneaded, set aside and allow to rest in a warm place for 30 minutes, until it has doubled in size.
- Roll the dough into a rectangle shape and cut into 1cm strips. Roll each strip into a thin, long sausage shape. Then coat each side with the melted butter. Transfer the bread stick onto the prepared baking tray. Spread wide apart.
- Bake for around 15–20 minutes or until golden.

Party Dips

Rainbow veggie trays are great for parties; they look great and taste fantastic. You can make funny faces, animals, spaceships or even a Minion out of the fruit and veggie on a tray, so get creative and see the kids tuck in. For inspirational ideas for rainbow fruit and veg trays see my website: www.mummaloveorganics.com.

Savoury Dips

CHEESY CHIVE DIP

Prep time: 5 minutes

4 heaped tbsp sour cream
3 tbsp fresh chives,
  chopped
1 tbsp grated Parmesan
1 tsp fresh lemon juice
pinch of salt

• Mix all the ingredients together in a bowl and serve!

SUNDRIED TOMATO DIP

Prep time: 5 minutes

40g sundried tomatoes
7 tbsp cream cheese
1 garlic clove, crushed
2 tbsp water
1 tbsp sour cream

• Pop in a blender until smooth and serve.

CAULIFLOWER CHEESE DIP

Prep time: 10 minutes
Cooking time: 30 minutes

**½ small cauliflower head,
  cut into small florets
3 tbsp rapeseed oil
salt and pepper
½ red onion, finely sliced
1 clove of garlic, crushed
8 tbsp mayonnaise
4 tbsp sour cream
1 tbsp cream cheese
2 tbsp grated Parmesan
50g grated cheese**

- Preheat the oven to 200°C/Gas Mark 6.
- Mix the cauliflower and 2 tbsp rapeseed oil in a bowl and season. Place the cauliflower on a baking tray and roast until golden (about 20-30 minutes). Turn the florets every 10 minutes or so.
- Whilst the cauliflower is cooking, place the rest of the oil in a frying pan and sauté the onion for 3 minutes. Add the garlic and cook for an extra minute. Carefully place the onion and garlic mixture into a food processor. Then add the mayonnaise, sour cream, cream cheese, Parmesan and grated cheese and pulse until smooth.
- Once the cauliflower is cooked, add to the blender with the other ingredients and blend until smooth. Serve immediately.

Sweet Dips

Fresh fruit is one of the best things to feed kids. Fruit is also easy to get kids to eat at parties, due to its natural sweetness. Trays of food art can be made with a vast array of fruit to encourage little ones to tantalise their taste buds. Fruits such as apple (sliced), strawberries, pineapple (in chunks or slices) and pear (sliced) are also great for dipping into fruity dips.

APPLE AND CINNAMON DIP

Prep time: 5 minutes

200g Greek yoghurt
1 red apple, cored and chopped
1 tbsp honey
½ tsp vanilla extract
½ tsp cinnamon

• Place all the ingredients into a blender and whizz until smooth. Serve immediately.

AVOCADO CHOCOLATE DIP

It might be wise not to mention the name of this one to the kids, at least not until they've tried (and loved) it!

Prep time: 5 minutes

1 avocado, peeled and stoned
1 banana
1 tbsp honey
2 tbsp Nutella

• Place all the ingredients in a bowl and blend together with a hand-held whisk until smooth. Serve straight away.

STRAWBERRY AND CREAM DIP

Prep time: 5 minutes

**7 fresh strawberries,
  chopped**
3 tbsp crème fraîche
2 tbsp marshmallow cream
1 tbsp Greek yoghurt
½ tsp vanilla extract

- Blend the strawberries in a bowl with a hand-held whisk. Remove and mix together with the other ingredients, then serve immediately.

Sandwiches

What's fun about sandwiches? Not a lot really. A sandwich is a sandwich, right? Wrong! Well, wrong if you cut it into fun shapes (using a cookie cutter) – kids absolutely love it! Shaped sandwiches are more likely to be tried by even fussy eaters. They do say we eat with our eyes, after all. Getting the kids to help make their own sandwich and choose the shape is also a good idea as it helps them get creative and encourages them to eat their masterpiece.

Healthy Sandwich Spreads

CHERRY DELIGHT

Prep time: 5 minutes

100g full-fat cream cheese
50g fresh cherries, chopped and pitted
1 tsp brown sugar

• Place the cream cheese, cherries and sugar into a blender and blend for a few minutes. Scoop the mixture into a lidded container. The mixture can then be kept in the fridge for up to 3 days.

GRATED APPLE AND CHEESE

Prep time: 5 minutes

1 apple, cored and grated
20g cheese, grated

• Mix the apple and cheese together . . .

COCONUT ALMOND BUTTER ....

Prep time: 15 minutes

250g raw almonds
50g coconut flesh
1 tsp honey

- Place almonds and coconut flesh into a blender and blend on high speed for around 15 minutes – until it is creamy. When you need to, stop blending and scrape the excess mixture on the sides of the blender into the main mix. Keep blending.
- Once the nuts have formed a creamy butter, add the honey and pulse one last time.
- Place in an airtight container and store in the fridge.

Kids' Sushi
Veg masquerading as yummy, different things to eat? It works!

HAM AND CUCUMBER ....

Prep time: 10 minutes

2 slices of bread
1 tbsp butter
**4 slices of cucumber, cut
into matchsticks**
**2 slices of ham, finely
shredded**

- Cut the crusts off the bread and flatten with a rolling pin. Butter the flattened bread. Lay the cucumber and the ham at the bottom of each slice.
- Roll up the bread, pressing gently to seal. Cut each roll into 4 equal pieces.

CARROT AND CHEESE ....

Prep time: 10 minutes

2 slices of bread
1 tbsp butter
10g grated cheese
10g grated carrot

- Cut the crusts off the bread and flatten with a rolling pin. Butter the flattened bread. Lay the cheese and the carrot at the bottom of each slice.
- Roll up the bread, pressing gently to seal. Cut each roll into 4 equal pieces.

Party Power Balls

These protein balls make great healthy party snacks as they are packed full of goodness as well as irresistible.

RAISIN DELIGHT

Makes 17
Prep time: 10 minutes
Chilling time: 35 minutes

40g cashew nuts
80g oats
70g raisins
120g Nutella

- Preheat oven to 200°C/Gas Mark 6.
- Roast the cashew nuts for 5 minutes before blending in a food processor.
- In a medium bowl, mix all of the ingredients together. Once the mixture is combined well, make 17 little round balls about 2.5cm wide. Place the balls on a tray with baking paper and refrigerate for around 30 minutes.

CHOCOLATE AND CRANBERRY BALLS

Makes 17
Prep time: 10 minutes
Chilling time: 30 minutes

50g oats
1 tbsp brown sugar
1 tsp vanilla extract
140g peanut butter
1 tbsp chia seeds
5 tbsp chocolate chips
50g dried cranberries

- In a medium bowl, mix all the ingredients together. Once the mixture is well combined, make 17 balls around 2.5cm wide. Place the balls on a tray with baking paper and refrigerate for around 30 minutes.

FRUIT AND NUT BALLS

Makes 17
Prep time: 10 minutes
Chilling time: 30 minutes

**50g oats
40g dried cranberries
1 tbsp chia seeds
40g chopped walnuts
40g raisins
180g peanut butter
1 tsp honey
1 tsp vanilla extract**

- Mix all of the ingredients together in a bowl. Once the mixture is combined well, make 17 little balls (around an inch wide). Place the balls on a tray with baking paper and refrigerate for around 30 minutes.

BLUEBERRY AND VANILLA MUFFINS

Whipping up a batch of tasty muffins is always a winner at parties. And sneaking in some fruit along the way is a bit of a win-win situation too!

Makes 12
Prep time: 10 minutes
Cooking time: 20 minutes

**180g plain flour
2 tsp baking powder
150g coconut sugar
110g butter, softened
1 medium egg
3 tbsp milk
1½ tsp vanilla extract
150g blueberries**

- Heat the oven to 190°C/Gas Mark 5 and prepare a standard-sized muffin tray with paper cake liners.
- In a bowl, mix the flour and baking powder. Add the sugar and butter and cream before adding the egg, milk and vanilla extract. Add the liquid mixture to the flour and combine with a whisk.
- Remove whisk and stir in the blueberries.
- Use a spatula to gently fold the blueberries into the mixture. Place a spoonful of mixture into each cake case.
- Place in the oven and bake the blueberry muffins for 15–20 minutes. Transfer the muffins to a cooling rack and let cool.

CARROT AND BANANA MUFFINS

Makes 12
Prep time: 10 minutes
Cooking time: 20 minutes

180g plain flour
150g coconut sugar (or
** granulated sugar)**
2 tsp baking powder
70ml rapeseed oil
1 medium egg
2 tbsp milk
1 tsp vanilla extract
1 small banana, mashed
100g carrot, grated

- Heat oven to 200°C/Gas Mark 6 and prepare a standard-size muffin tray with paper cake liners.
- In a bowl, mix together the flour, coconut sugar and baking powder. Put the oil in a measuring jug and whisk in the egg, milk and vanilla extract. Add the liquid mixture to the flour and sugar and combine with a whisk.
- Add the banana and whisk with a hand-held whisk to a smooth consistency. Using a spatula, gently fold the carrot into the mixture.
- Place in the oven and bake for 15–20 minutes. Transfer the muffins to a cooling rack.

MANGO AND COCONUT MUFFINS

Makes 12
Prep time: 10 minutes
Cooking time: 20 minutes

180g plain flour
150g coconut sugar (or
** granulated sugar)**
2 tsp baking powder
50ml rapeseed oil
1 medium egg
1 tsp vanilla extract
50g mango, mashed
100g shredded coconut

- Heat the oven to 200°C/Gas Mark 6. Prepare a standard-size muffin tray with paper cake liners.
- In a bowl, mix the flour, coconut sugar and baking powder. Then add the oil to a measuring jug and whisk in the egg and vanilla extract.
- Add the liquid mixture to the flour and sugar and combine with a whisk. Add the mango, mash, then add the coconut.
- Place in the oven and bake the muffins for 15–20 minutes. Transfer the muffins to a cooling rack.

BEETROOT COOKIES

These fab beetroot cookies involve a root vegetable that is a true superfood on its own. Beets are packed full of vitamins and minerals, as well as being overloaded with antioxidants. They truly are an ideal food to keep your kids active throughout the day.

Makes 20
Prep time: 10 minutes
Cooking time: 15 minutes

220g butter
220g sugar
220g plain flour
1 tbsp baking powder
1 medium beetroot, grated
1 tbsp vanilla extract
100g chocolate chips

- Preheat the oven to 190ºC/Gas Mark 5.
- Cream the butter together with the sugar. Sieve the flour and baking powder and add to the mix.
- Add the beetroot and vanilla extract and mix well. Then add the chocolate chips and give it another good mix.
- Using a spoon, place small dollops of the mixture onto a baking tray lined with baking paper. Make sure they are spread apart – you may need to bake the cookies in batches.
- Bake for 12–14 minutes.

CHOCOLATE CLEMENTINES

This little clementine snack is easy to make, deliciously addictive, and the cutest little party appetiser.

Prep time: 15 minutes
Chilling time: 15 minutes

½ Terry's Chocolate Orange
5 clementines, peeled and
**   segmented**

- Line a baking tray with greaseproof paper.
- Gently melt the Chocolate Orange in a glass bowl set on a saucepan half-filled with boiling water, stirring constantly.
- One by one, dip the clementine segments into the chocolate and transfer to the greaseproof paper. Once all of the pieces have been dipped, place the tray in the fridge for 15 minutes.

FRUIT LOLLIES

Homemade lollies are a healthy alternative to the sugar-filled shop-bought kind. They are not only packed full of nutrients, they taste great too.

Makes 6
Prep time: 15 minutes
Freezing time: 6 hours

3 kiwi fruits, peeled and sliced
150g strawberries, quartered
150g raspberries, halved
100g mango, cut into small chunks
200ml coconut water
Lollipop moulds

- Fill 6 moulds with fruit (but don't push it in) making sure there is space between the pieces.
- Now fill each mould with the coconut water and freeze for around 6 hours, or until solid.

Fruity Kebabs

The ideal way of getting your kids to eat 5-a-day! Pop some fruit on a stick!! An excellent idea is to cut food into hearts or stars. It makes these healthy treats extra-attractive.

Makes 6
Prep time: 5 minutes

SUMMER DELIGHT

12 raspberries
12 strawberries
1 clementine, segmented
12 green grapes, deseeded
   and halved
12 pieces of chopped
   mango

TROPICAL TASTE

2 kiwi fruits, cut into chunks
12 pineapple chunks
12 green grapes, deseeded
   and halved
1 tangerine, segmented

STRAWBERRY SURPRISE ....

Kids love everything about chocolate-covered strawberries. They love the crunchy melt-in-your-mouth shell and the cool, sweet strawberry beneath, making them an ideal party treat.

Prep time: 20 minutes
Chilling time: 15 minutes

150g strawberries
200g white chocolate
jar of milk chocolate
  sprinkles

- Wash the strawberries and remove their stalks. Gently melt the white chocolate in a glass bowl set on a saucepan half-filled with boiling water, stirring constantly.
- One by one, dip the strawberries into the chocolate. Add some of the milk chocolate sprinkles and transfer to baking tray covered in greaseproof paper.
- Once all the pieces have been dipped, place the tray in the fridge for 15 minutes.

Drinks

Drinks and birthday parties go hand in hand, but rather than high-sugar drinks try these healthier alternatives.

PINK LEMONADE WITH REAL RASPBERRIES

Prep time: 10 minutes
Cooking time: 10 minutes

200g sugar
125ml coconut water
250ml water
100g raspberries
100g strawberries
100ml freshly squeezed
   lemon juice
1 litre sparkling water

- Combine the sugar, coconut water and water in a small saucepan. Keep the heat on low, stir until the sugar has dissolved.
- While the syrup is cooking, purée the fresh raspberries and strawberries. Once they are puréed, squish them through a sieve to separate the seeds from the juice.
- Pour the lemon and raspberry juice into a large glass jug.
- Once the syrup is ready, pour it into the jug of fruit juice. Add 1 litre of sparkling water to dilute.
- Stir and enjoy!

MANGO JUICE

Prep time: 5 minutes

1 mango, peeled and cut
   into small chunks
500ml coconut water

- Blend the mango and the coconut water in a blender. Place into a jug, add ice cubes and serve.

PARTY PUNCH

Prep time: 5 minutes

1 small pineapple, cut into
small chunks
200g strawberries, stalks
removed and fruit
quartered
100g raspberries
½ litre cranberry and
raspberry juice
1 litre sparkling water

• Put the fruit into a large glass bowl, pour
in the juice and sparkling water and serve.

9
SUPERFOODS FOR KIDS

In countries like the United Kingdom, people enjoy an extensive choice of healthy foods and increasingly convenient ways to shop. And yet, despite this choice and convenience, we find soaring obesity rates among both adults and kids, and serious, preventable conditions such as type 2 diabetes are becoming endemic within the population.

Only a few generations ago, people shopped at local shops and markets and bought foods that had been grown organically at local farms and orchards. Even though shoppers had far fewer choices and far less convenience, you could say that by choosing fresh, tasty, nutritious, unprocessed foods, they were actually buying 'superfoods'! Preservatives used back then were likely to be natural products such as salt, sugar and vinegar, and foods did not contain 'numbers' or mysterious substances with unpronounceable names. A family would usually sit down together at mealtimes and babies were given a puréed portion of the same meal. Mention the phrase 'fussy eaters' when describing your children and people would have probably stared at you blankly and with slight confusion. For the current generation of children, being a 'fussy eater' is the norm. If you say your child is a 'happy eater' (i.e. an 'unfussy eater') people will probably stare at you blankly and with great confusion!

'Really? Your child is *happy* to try new tastes? Your child is *happy* to eat a *variety* of nutritious foods? How can that possibly be! What have you *done* to your child?'

Today's images of people shopping for food and feeding their families paint pictures of stress and misery. Yes, misery! You only have to stand in a checkout queue for less than a minute at one of the large discount supermarkets (I won't mention any names) to feel everyone's tension levels mounting to insufferable proportions. As people line up silently behind your back, you edge slowly towards the cashier who may/may not greet you with a smile/grimace (delete as appropriate). Then, as your produce is rapidly scanned through, it begins to mount up on the counter, prompting you to hurriedly toss everything into your trolley – yes, even the tomatoes! – to avoid WASTING A NANO SECOND OF ANYONE ELSE'S TIME. (Phew! I feel stressed just writing that paragraph.)

Just as we pack our days with more and more work, activities and commitments that sometimes keep us awake into the early hours, so do we cram our shopping trolleys with frozen foods and microwaveable meals as we race through our weekly (or even monthly) supermarket 'sweep'. With ever-increasing irony, we sit at home and tuck into our ready meals and fast-food takeaways while watching the latest celebrity chef on television demonstrating how to concoct easy, healthy, delicious home-cooked meals!

SUPERFOODS FOR KIDS

The idea of 'superfoods for kids' is quite simply an approach using fresh, tasty, unprocessed foods that offer a wealth of nutrients for optimum health and vitality. Could anything be simpler than a protein-rich omelette thrown together over the hob using a few fresh eggs and some chopped veg such as tomatoes, onions and green beans? And if they ask, 'What's for pudding, Mum?' you can dazzle their taste buds with a sweet fruit salad topped with a dollop of tangy yoghurt. It's all about nourishing our cheeky little ones to keep them healthy while they play, learn and develop into healthy (and often cheekier!) big ones!

GOOD MOOD FOODS

We all want our children to be healthy – and happy. Offering them a balanced diet of wholesome, unprocessed foods is one of the key ways in which you can ensure health of both body and mind. Food = Mood. Coincidentally, the words rhyme. However, the interconnections between the food we eat and our subsequent behaviours and moods extend far beyond simple linguistic comparisons. 'We are what we eat' is a well-worn phrase, but it still rings oh-so-true.

For example, parents regularly notice negative changes in the behaviours and energy levels of their children during or after events such as birthday parties. Children's birthday parties are often occasions where kids eat greater-than-usual quantities of foods and drinks that are laden with fat, sugar, salt, caffeine and additives. Parents notice that their otherwise well-behaved offspring suddenly become 'hyper' – that is, they become inattentive, unwilling to follow any sensible instructions and display behaviours that are erratic and uncontrolled. There are clear scientific reasons for these sudden changes in behaviour and mood, one of which is a surge in blood sugar levels, which is shortly followed by a 'crash'. Tiredness is not the only reason why you might be taking home a horridly irritable child once the party has finished! In the short term, an occasional binge on traditional party foods such as crisps, biscuits, cakes and sweets (in other words 'junk food') won't place your child at severe risk of delinquency. However, in the long term, regularly eating 'junk' in place of healthier options could adversely affect your child's moods, behaviours, concentration span, energy levels and rate of learning. The simple carbohydrates found in junk foods can have a detrimental effect on your child's schooling by reducing concentration levels and the ability to cooperate with others. In fact, junk food has been linked to increased hyperactivity in children, as noted in a 2009 study published by the *European Journal of Clinical Nutrition*.

DITCH THE JUNK

It goes without saying that you love your kids and want the best for them. So why not ditch junk foods and offer superfoods instead? Yes, it's easy to open up a packet of biscuits or bag of crisps for your kids when they need a snack; however, with just a tiny amount of planning and preparation, you can offer them something that will nourish their growing bodies and keep their moods on an even keel. Superfoods are typically high in healthful goodies such as vitamins and minerals and low in not-so-healthy ingredients such as food additives, sugar and saturated fats.

Frequent consumption of junk foods containing high amounts of fat and sugar can lead to obesity, which can bring serious consequences for physical and mental health. Children need to be physically active to help their growing bodies develop coordination and muscular strength. Obese children might struggle to join in successfully with some physical activities – either in or out of school. Children who are overweight can also experience poor posture and health problems such as backache and painful joints, all of which can contribute to feelings of low self-esteem and even depression.

Reducing your child's intake of junk foods literally makes room in his or her tummy for those uber-nourishing alternatives! It's all about nurturing healthier, happier children. Simple. A balanced diet that's low in junk-food 'baddies' offers optimum nourishment, helping to stabilise children's blood-sugar levels and, as a consequence, their behaviour and moods too.

CUT OUT CAFFEINE

Children are likely to be more susceptible than the majority of adults to the effects of caffeine on the nervous system, with possible symptoms ranging from jittery behaviour to nausea, stomach aches and headaches. Caffeine is not only found in beverages such as tea, coffee and energy drinks – which are not usually offered to children – but also in foods and drinks like chocolate and cola, which some children might consume on a regular basis. Furthermore, chocolate and cola often contain high levels of sugar and acids, such as phosphoric acid, which can contribute to dental decay and erosion of tooth enamel.

OMEGA-3 FATTY ACIDS

In recent years, fats have become much maligned in our culture, with the expectation that we should all follow the low-fat trail towards a completely fat-free diet utopia! However, just as we need proteins for growth, and carbohydrates for energy, our bodies also require fats. Fats are especially important for fast-growing children as they support cell growth and provide an essential source of energy. Fats enable the body to absorb nutrients like vitamins A and D and to produce certain hormones. Fats also help protect the body's vital organs and keep us warm. Of course, we should all try to limit our intake of saturated fats, which are found in foods such as fatty meats, hard cheeses, pastries and cakes. But one of the most important areas of research into how foods affect children's behaviour has seen that oily fish containing beneficial omega-3 fatty acids can help stabilise mood swings and generally improve the concentration levels, behaviour and learning abilities of children with ADHD. If your child does not like oily fish, or follows a vegetarian diet, it might be worth consulting your doctor to discuss any potential benefits of omega-3 supplements.

Sources of omega-3 include:
- oily fish (for example, salmon and mackerel)
- walnuts
- linseeds and flaxseeds
- omega-3-enriched eggs

BE ADDITIVE-AWARE

Food additives, such as artificial colours, artificial flavourings and preservatives, are commonly found in processed foods. They are added to foods to enhance colours, flavours and textures and to delay food spoilage and prolong shelf life. Despite the fact that some types of additives have already been banned in some countries, many are still in use, and we should continue to regard them with caution. Commonly available synthetic food additives have been linked to the development of conditions such as allergies and migraines in susceptible children.

Synthetic food additives that are best avoided include:
- tartrazine (E102)
- quinoline yellow (E104)
- sunset yellow (E110)
- carmosine (E122)
- ponceau 4R (E124)
- allura red (E129)
- sodium benzoate (E211)

FOLLOW THE RAINBOW!

Why eat foods that have been artificially coloured? It's completely bizarre! 'Mumma Nature' has made it easy for us all to gain optimum nourishment by eating a variety of rainbow-coloured fruit and veg. Fruits and vegetables in the colours red, orange, yellow, green, blue and purple contain a variety of nutrients that function as antioxidants to support healthy growth and help prevent diseases that are caused by cell-damaging free radicals. Some of these antioxidants are abundant within fruit and veg of a certain colour. But what are antioxidants? And what are free radicals?

ANTIOXIDANTS V FREE RADICALS

Here's a 'sciencey' chunk, but I'll try to keep it simple.

Free radicals are atoms or groups of atoms that contain an unpaired electron. (Electrons usually come in pairs.) Free radicals form in the body when oxygen interacts with certain molecules and this can start a chain reaction that causes cell damage within the body. Free radicals may cause cells to function poorly or die and, in some instances, trigger diseases such as cancer.

Antioxidants are molecules that help balance out the process by donating electrons to neutralise the harmful effects of free radicals. Key nutrients that function as antioxidants, such as vitamins C and A, cannot be made by the body but must be supplied by foods. A 'rainbow diet' comprising a variety of fruit and vegetables provides vital antioxidants to help keep us healthy. (You could say antioxidants are superheroes disguised as fruit and veg!)

Reds

Red fruits and vegetables like tomatoes, red peppers, watermelon and red cabbage contain a plant pigment called lycopene. Red apples and red onions contain healthful amounts of quercetin. Lycopene and quercetin are both antioxidant superstars!

Sneaky recipe hints for *red-hued superfood*!

- Apples: can help sweeten a gluten-free pancake
- Beetroot: can be made into crisps, blended into soups, cake mixtures and cookie dough
- Cherries: try them in sandwiches with cream cheese and apple
- Raspberries and strawberries: purée into a naturally sweet sauce to pour over tangy yoghurt
- Sweet red peppers: slice onto pizza, purée into savoury sauces or chop into sticks for dipping
- Tomatoes: use for curries, dips, sauces and pizza toppings
- Watermelon: remove seeds, freeze cubes of fruit and then pop into drinks of water

Yellows and Oranges

Citrus fruits, such as lemons, oranges and grapefruits are rich in vitamin C. Yellow and orange-coloured produce such as carrots, yellow and orange peppers, and squash are high in beta-carotene, a precursor of vitamin A, or retinol, which can be turned into vitamin A in the body if needed. Vitamin C and beta-carotene strengthen the immune system and have important antioxidant properties.

Sneaky recipe hints for *yellow-* and *orange-hued superfood*!

- Apricots: chop and stir into mild curries and cake mixtures or blend into jam
- Bananas: mash and add to a cake or pancake mix or make banana bread
- Carrots: mash with potatoes for toppings or grate and add to cake mixtures, cookie dough, pasta sauces, pizza toppings and soups
- Mangoes: combine with oranges for a delicious fresh juice
- Oranges: freeze the juice in lolly moulds for refreshing ice lollies
- Peaches: dice and mix into breakfast cereal just before serving
- Squash: slice into batons, toss in olive oil and seasoning, then bake as 'French fries'
- Swedes: mash, mash, mash! (Then mix with any other veg!)
- Sweetcorn: cut cooked cobs into sections and push onto skewers for sweetcorn 'lollies'
- Sweet potatoes: use as you would white potatoes – roasted, mashed, fried . . .

Greens

Dark-green vegetables such as broccoli and green leafy veg such as spinach offer a wealth of essential nutrients, including vitamin K, folic acid, potassium, magnesium and lutein, all of which contribute to good health and perform antioxidant functions within the body.

Sneaky recipe hints for *green-hued superfood*!

- Asparagus: the ultimate, luxury finger foods – great for dipping!
- Avocados: mash up into a chocolate pudding
- Broccoli: add to homemade burgers, shepherd's pie or curry
- Cucumber: chop off a chunk, wash, peel and then eat like an apple
- Courgettes: purée into sauces, mash into cakes or 'spiralize' and use like spaghetti
- Kale: ideal for vegetable crisps
- Kiwi fruit: ideal for smoothies and for ice-lolly mixtures
- Pears: try roasted with a dollop of vanilla-flavoured yoghurt
- Peas: cook and mash into a 'pea pesto' and spread onto crunchy crostini

- Spinach: combine with orange juice and whizz to make a green smoothie
- Cress: grow your own from seeds planted in cleaned-out eggshells to make 'cress heads'! Then chop into eggy sandwiches!

Blues and Purples

Anthocyanins are pigments that give produce such as blackcurrants, blueberries, aubergines and purple-sprouting broccoli their gorgeous blue and purple colours. Anthocyanins have strong antioxidant properties.

Sneaky recipe hints for *blue-* and *purple-hued superfood*!

- Aubergine: when roasted, purée into sauces, slice onto pizzas or chop into homemade burgers
- Blackberries: blend into smoothies and then freeze to make popsicles
- Blueberries: their firmness makes them ideal for fruity kebabs. Squish for little children (choking hazard).
- Plums: chop and add to couscous with apples and lemon juice for a light salad

SUPERFOOD SEEDS

The seed family comprises grains, nuts, beans and, of course, seeds! For example, grains such as wheat and oats are grass seeds. Nuts such as hazelnuts and almonds are seeds from trees, while beans such as soya beans and chickpeas are seeds that come from plants called legumes. We tend to refer to smaller types of seeds like poppy seeds and sunflower seeds (which derive from flowering plants) as just 'seeds'.

Mini definitions now done, let's consider the nutritional importance of seeds and why they should be included as part of a child's healthy diet. Small is beautiful! Seeds are little superfood powerhouses packed with carbohydrates, protein, fibre, unsaturated fats and an array of essential vitamins and minerals.

Here's a by-no-means-definitive list – a 'taster', if you like – to describe just a few of the myriad types of superfood seeds Mumma Nature has provided for us!

Amaranth
Similar in size to poppy seeds, amaranth seeds provide a tasty, gluten-free alternative to oats when making porridge.

Barley
A nutrient-packed wholegrain, barley makes a delicious alternative to rice in dishes such as risotto. You can also add it to vegetable soups to make them a bit more filling.

Beans
Full of protein and soluble fibre, bean varieties include black-eyed beans, butter beans and cannellini beans. Blend them into sauces or add them to savoury dishes such as lasagna and cottage pie.

Brown Rice
Unlike white rice, brown rice is a wholegrain with its outer hull intact. Therefore it offers more fibre than white rice, along with an array of essential nutrients. It has a slightly chewy texture and nutty taste and you can use it to replace white rice in any dish you like – even rice pudding! Whip up a comforting pud using brown rice, almond milk, a handful of raisins and a pinch of cinnamon.

Buckwheat
Flour made from buckwheat seeds can be used instead of wheat flour for many recipes. Why not use it to make delicious gluten-free pancakes?

Chia Seeds
Blend a handful of these tiny black seeds into a fruity breakfast smoothie to boost your child's intake of protein and omega-3 essential fatty acids – all set for a busy day at school.

Chickpeas
Children often love the 'dip, lick and crunch' delights of a little bowl of hummus served with fresh veggie batons, such as sticks of carrot and cucumber.

Lentils
Brown, green, yellow and red – lentils come in a variety of colours, but they all provide similar health-giving benefits. They are high in

protein, dietary fibre, vitamins and minerals. These colourful little seeds are so versatile, and they offer a tasty alternative to fatty meats like mince in hearty dishes such as shepherd's pie and spaghetti bolognese.

Oats

There is so much more to oats than porridge! And yet, for sustained and slow energy release in the form of complex carbs, along with protein and B vitamins, a bowl of milky porridge oats ticks all the boxes, including those of warmth, taste and comfort.

Quinoa

Quinoa is packed with protein and these nutritious, gluten-free seeds lend themselves to a wealth of recipes. Sprinkle onto salads, toss into a smoothie or blend with chopped veg for veggie burgers with subtle texture and crunch . . .

Teff

Teff consist of tiny gluten-free seeds that pack a serious punch beyond their weight as they are full of protein, vitamins and minerals. Ivory teff tastes milder than brown teff, which has a slightly richer, nuttier and more 'chocolatey' taste. Delicious in savoury dishes and for sweet treats.

Protein Power

Fast-growing children need sufficient daily portions of protein foods such as eggs, beans, meat, poultry and fish. Choose lean meats to cut back on saturated fat and buy organic varieties where you can. Fish has superfood status: it's rich in protein and low in fat and it contains a wealth of vitamins and minerals. Fish is also easy to digest and it cooks relatively quickly too – priceless for those times when your already impatient toddler is on the verge of hunger meltdown!

10
MEAL PLANNING

Meal planning has a number of benefits, and, once you understand how to do it so that it's no longer a chore, it can help hugely with mealtimes. So what are the benefits of meal planning?

HEALTHY EATING

Eating healthily is essential to maintain the body's natural balance. However, in order to do it right – every time – it takes proper planning. Meal planning offers you the chance to work out exactly what it is you need to stay healthy before you even reach the supermarket; you know what healthy meals your family will enjoy in the coming week. And if you have just switched over to a healthy diet, then planning is perhaps even more important, as having the right food in the house and using it for a purpose will make sticking to your new regime easier.

FOOD WASTAGE

Food planning absolutely prevents food wastage. It can be fun (if that's the right word!) to go to the supermarket and browse, picking up bits and pieces as we go and reassuring ourselves that we are going to use everything we buy . . . but how many times has this happened only for you to throw away much of it because it just wasn't used? If you plan the meals in advance and only buy what you absolutely need to buy, you won't waste anything – everything will be used. And it will be cheaper too!

STRESS (LESS)

There is enough stress in our day-to-day lives without adding to it by panicking over what to cook. Realising that the children will be getting hungry and that you've got no idea what to feed them is a major stress factor, but having a simple meal plan in place will reduce that to nothing. Kids hungry? Great, you know exactly what you're going to feed them to ensure they get the nutrients and healthy stuff they need. No more uncertainty, no more hastily cobbled together meals that aren't as good for them as they should be. No more guilt.

THE PLAN

Below is a simple plan to get you started – change it in any way you like, as long as you know in advance what everyone is going to eat. It will save you so much time, money and worry!

Week 1

Day	Breakfast	Lunch	Dinner
Monday	Banana Pancakes	Veggie Wrap	Cowboy Casserole
Tuesday	Apricot and Cranberry Cereal Bar	Grated Apple and Cheese sandwich	Crafty Carbonara
Wednesday	Berry Explosion Milkshake	Banana Rama sushi sandwich	Brilliant Bean Burgers
Thursday	Porridge – Pink or Green	Egg and Cress sandwich	See-in-the Dark Chicken
Friday	Dippy egg and soldiers	Strawberry Sensation	Cheesy Meatballs
Saturday	Morning Glory smoothie	Veggie Patties	Pasta dish with a sneaky sauce
Sunday	Special Baked Beans on Toast	Cherry Delight spread with wholemeal bagel	Roast Chicken with Cauliflower Mash and Carrot Chips

Week 2

Day	Breakfast	Lunch	Dinner
Monday	Strawberry Surprise Pancakes	Chicken Wrap	Sweet Shepherd's Pie
Tuesday	Teddy's Blueberry Toast	Nut Butter with a wholemeal bagel	Chicken and Vegetable Pasta Bake
Wednesday	Tropical Fruit Salad	Grated Apple and Cheese sandwich	Hidden Veggie Quiche
Thursday	Granola	Fruity Delight	Homemade Fish Fingers
Friday	Wholemeal toast with Strawberry and Apricot spread	Lunch Kabobs	Marvellous Mushroom Risotto
Saturday	Mango Mania smoothie	Rainbow Couscous	Lasagne
Sunday	Dippy egg and soldiers	Banana and Cinnamon sandwich	Salmon and Cauliflower and Broccoli Cheese

Week 3

Day	Breakfast	Lunch	Dinner
Monday	Coconut Dream smoothie	Egg and Cress sandwich	Dino The Dinosaur's Favourite Dish
Tuesday	Strawberries and Cream smoothie	Veggie Wrap	Coconut Dahl
Wednesday	Banana Pancakes	Oatmeal and Cranberry Energy Ball	Fruity Chicken
Thursday	Granola	Broccoli and Cheese Muffins	Marvellous Macaroni
Friday	Berry Explosion Milkshake	Cheese and Ham sandwich	Fabulous Fish Pie
Saturday	Wholemeal toast and marmite	Tortilla Pizzas	Homemade Pot Noodle
Sunday	Tropical Fruit Salad	Marmite and cheese sandwich	Sneaky Spag Bol

Week 4

Day	Breakfast	Lunch	Dinner
Monday	Dippy egg and soldiers	Veg platter and dips	Nachos Packed with Veggies
Tuesday	Porridge – Pink or Green	Mango Mania smoothie	Creamy Tuna Pasta Bake
Wednesday	Apple Delight Bites	Three-Cheese Pasta	Salmon Fishcakes
Thursday	Hot Quinoa Cereal	Salmon and cream cheese on a wholemeal bagel	Very Best Vegetable Pie
Friday	Wholemeal toast and Homemade Peanut Butter	Egg and cress sandwich	Rainbow Salad
Saturday	Berry Crunch	Peanut Butter and Banana Rice Cakes	Spinach and Ricotta Pasta
Sunday	Granola	Courgette Fritters	Veggie Quinoa

Now remember, this is just a guide. It can be changed. Breakfasts and lunches can often be a bit more fluid and changed around as needed, but with dinners it's best to stick with what you have planned if at all possible. Sometimes it's not, of course, because that's life!

You know what your children like best, and what will work for them. Perhaps they've had a long day and just need a bit of comfort food. Maybe they are up for something new and you can try them with a different dish.

You'll notice there are no snacks on the menu planner and that's because not all children want or need them. If yours do, then fruit is always a good option. And 3 p.m., or just after school, is a good time for them to have one as they are often hungry at this time but it's still going to be a little way until dinner.

FINAL THOUGHTS

Congratulations! You 'sneaky mums' out there should be proud of yourselves because parenting is hard and good parenting is even harder. By taking control of what your children are eating and ensuring that they are getting all the nutrients and goodness they need to thrive, you're doing an excellent job. And, hopefully, these recipes will give your children an appreciation for great, healthy food, and encourage them to explore new tastes and flavours.

I totally believe that the recipes in this book will eliminate unhealthy eating habits, give your children more creative – and therefore more interesting – yet healthy meals and bond families over food whilst creating healthy-eating habits to last a lifetime. I really hope this book becomes a well-used, cherished, informative and useful tool in your kitchen.

Please keep in touch through www.mummaloveorganics.com and my Instagram account mummaloveorganics_. Also, watch out for my YouTube channel, Mum's Sneaky Recipes!

REFERENCES

Chapter 2: Beaming Breakfasts

The Food Doctor: Healing Foods for Mind and Body by Ian Marber, Collins & Brown Ltd, 2004.

Chapter 3: Superb Snacks

http://www.andjrnl.org/article/S2212-2672(13)00304-3/abstract (The addition of a plain or herb-flavored reduced-fat dip is associated with improved preschoolers' intake of vegetables) (2016)

http://kidshealth.org/en/parents/snacking.html

Chapter 5: Devious Dinners

http://thefamilydinnerproject.org/resources/faq/

http://www.organicfacts.net/health-benefits/other/adzuki-beans.html

http://www.whfoods.com/genpage.php?tname=foodspice&dbid=64

http://www.momjunction.com/articles/benefits-of-carrots-for-kids_00355279/

http://www.wholeliving.com/134734/power-foods-butternut-squash

http://www.indiaparenting.com/childs-healthcare/53_5814/health-benefits-of-almonds-for-kids.html

http://www.symptomfind.com/nutrition-supplements/health-benefits-of-tuna/

https://www.hawaiifamilyforum.org/legacy-of/

Chapter 7: Gluten-Free

https://www.coeliac.org.uk/gluten-free-diet-and-lifestyle/gf-diet/

Chapter 8: Party Foods

http://www.thehealthsite.com/fitness/health-benefits-of-chicken-sa214/

Chapter 9: Superfood For Kids

http://www.ncbi.nlm.nih.gov/pmc/articles/PMC2664919/
(Junk food diet and childhood behavioural problems: Results from the ALSPAC cohort)

http://www.webmd.com/food-recipes/how-food-affects-your-moods

http://www.bbcgoodfood.com/howto/guide/behaviour-children-food-and-additives

http://www.dermalinstitute.com/uk/library/22_article_What_Is_A_Free_Radical_.html

https://heartmdinstitute.com/diet-nutrition/antioxidants-and-free-radicals

http://www.momjunction.com/articles/garlic-for-kids_00365608/

https://woolworthsbabyandtoddlerclub.com.au/toddler/toddlers-health-and-nutrition/why-blueberries-are-good-for-your-toddler/

http://www.tandfonline.com/doi/abs/10.1080/09540260600583031
www.parentinghealthybabies.com

The Food Doctor by Vicki Edgson and Ian Marber, Collins & Brown Ltd, 2004.

Healing Foods by Neal's Yard Remedies, Dorling Kindersley, 2013.

INDEX